Praise for *Advice is for Winners:*
How to Get Advice for Better Decisions in Life and Work

This is not your father's self-help book. Valdes-Perez expertly weaves humorous and endearing anecdotes with compelling research on the importance of asking for advice. You will be amazed at what you learn, and you will come away with a new approach toward making all types of life's decisions. My advice: read the book!

— MARK J. MORRISSETTE, Managing Director, North Atlantic Capital

Advice is for Winners clearly and thoughtfully addresses a topic that is too often underappreciated and misunderstood. Building on his diverse experiences, the author brings credibility and powerful insights about advice and how to use it. Audiences from students to professionals will find this "advice on advice" to be extremely valuable.

— EDEN FISHER, Professor of the Practice, Engineering
and Public Policy, Carnegie Mellon University

Great advice in plain English from the winner who founded and ran one of the most successful high-tech companies in Pittsburgh's history, sold to IBM in 2012. I have one piece of advice for you: read this book!

— OREN ETZIONI, founder of four technology companies and
Washington Research Foundation Entrepreneurship Professor,
University of Washington

You had better read this book if you want to make smarter decisions, especially the decisions that keep you awake at night. This well-written resourceful guide should be required reading for anyone who values great outcomes and a good night's sleep. If only he had written this much sooner!

— ANNE C. MCCAFFERTY, Mother of Two and Hirer of Hundreds

Advice is for Winners turns into a skill something that has so far been considered an art. The author's narrative style and numerous practical examples make the book fascinating reading. I had also the pleasure to listen to his lecture on the topic. He is not only an excellent writer -- he is also a great story teller and a passionate speaker. Highly recommended!

— MAREK DRUZDZEL, Associate Professor, School of
Information Sciences, University of Pittsburgh

No one knows it all. The winners are those who know when to seek advice, how and where to look for it, and how to interpret it. Valdes-Perez provides an insightful look into why so many of us often fail to put this seemingly mundane observation to practice. This book is a truly compelling read for anyone seeking to improve their decision making in life and work. As an entrepreneur myself, I strongly recommend it to anyone undertaking something new and challenging.

— NORMAN M. SADEH, co-founder and Chairman of Wombat Security
Technologies and Professor, Carnegie Mellon University

We all, at times, can miss the forest for the trees. Mr. Valdes-Perez embarks on a simple but important journey that can keep us grounded – developing the humility and awareness to ask for advice and the wisdom to know when and how to ask well.

— FREDERICK W. THIEMAN, President, Buhl Foundation

Advice is for Winners is an invaluable career resource for students seeking internships or fulltime jobs. Dr. Valdes-Perez provides practical tips for utilizing this important but often overlooked source of information (and uses his own experiences as a new graduate as illustrations of how powerful the right words of advice can be). No matter what field or profession that you are choosing to pursue as you begin a career, *Advice is for Winners* is a must-read.

— KEVIN COLLINS, Assistant Director, Career and Professional
Development Center, Carnegie Mellon University

As an avid reader of personal and professional development books, this book is the first to really delve into the question "Why don't we seek advice" when it would be so beneficial to do so. This book answers that question and provides great suggestions on how we can become much better advice-seekers.

— DAVE COHEN, Senior Business Consultant
and Executive Board, Beth El Congregation

Raul, a committed, intensely focused entrepreneur, who built a company from a noble idea to a successful exit with IBM, has written about the pragmatic and overlooked notion of advice. It is often a lonely journey building a technology company. Raul offers practical wisdom which is highly valuable for anyone in the business of designing and deploying technology solutions.

— AUDREY RUSSO, President and CEO, Pittsburgh Technology Council

Raul practices what he preaches in this book. As an advisor to my start-up technology company, not only has Raul offered experienced sound advice, but he has also instilled in me a deep sense of the essential importance and value of proactively seeking advice.

> — ALON LAVIE, founder and CEO, Safaba Translation Solutions and
> President, Association for Machine Translation in the Americas (2008-2012)

As a new MBA student, the first thing we are taught by peers and career counselors is how to network and quickly build a relationship for the sole purpose of landing the next job. *Advice is for Winners*, on the other hand, helps you find the right mentor and build meaningful life-long professional relationships that will help you learn from their experience and spur your long-term professional growth. A must read for an MBA and an aspiring MBA.

> — TANMAY SINHA, MBA student, Tepper School of Business
> Carnegie Mellon University

Mr. Valdes-Perez has finally put into words what most of us have experienced-making a wrong decision because we didn't seek advice. His insight is astounding and refreshing. This book reveals the importance of working with others and listening to others to create the best result possible. He has captured the true essence of the phrase "no man is an island" and guides the reader to a formula of success- particularly in a global economy.

> — LOURDES SANCHEZ-RIDGE, former Assistant U.S. Attorney and
> President, Pittsburgh Metropolitan Area Hispanic Chamber of Commerce

Raul Valdes-Perez offers up winning advice for tackling the important decisions we face in our day-to-day lives. Whether it's your personal or work life, *Advice for Winners* offers a common sense approach to making better choices. This is a must-read book for anyone interested in making better decisions.

> — RICHARD LUNAK, President and CEO, Innovation Works

A much-needed guide for would-be winners at all stages, from adolescence to retirement. Highly recommended!

> — S. THOMAS EMERSON, The David T. and Lindsay J. Morgenthaler
> Distinguished Career Professor of Entrepreneurship,
> Carnegie Mellon University

ADVICE IS FOR WINNERS: How to Get Advice for Better Decisions in Life and Work

RAUL VALDES-PEREZ

Copyright © 2012 by Raul Valdes-Perez
All rights reserved.

ISBN: 978-0615709208

Ganador Press, Pittsburgh, Pennsylvania

ACKNOWLEDGMENTS

A book on self reliance could be conceived and written in a cave. But a book on inter-reliance - this one - should owe its existence to a community of friends, colleagues, and acquaintances that lend their ears and offer encouragement, ideas, pointers, introductions, stories, alerts, and how-to instructions - in short, advice. Such has been my case. I express my gratitude to the following people.

Anne McCafferty for her encouragement, for being the first reader of an early draft, and for perceptively recommending a re-ordering of the chapters, among other suggestions.

Dave Cohen for reading the entire draft in detail and making valuable writing and topic suggestions.

Liliana Garnica for her suggestion of other reasons why people avoid seeking advice and for sharing her own college story.

Maria Valdes-Perez for suggesting a chapter on What Major Should I Study?

Audrey Russo for suggesting a chapter on Should I Change Jobs?

John McCormick for general encouragement and suggesting the link to adolescent biology.

William Von Hagen for early discussions of book publishing in general and for pointing out cases that made their way into the book.

Rebeca Dosal, for suggesting interesting people to discuss advice-seeking with.

Fred Thiemann for clarifying the relationship to business networking.

Sam Deep, Robert Fragasso, and Razi Imam for sharing their own book-publishing experiences.

Ariadna Font for her encouragement and advice on how to consider the impact of the web and social networking technologies.

Bruce McLaren for pointers to relevant academic work.

Tom Sands for agreeing to share the story of his hiring at Vivisimo as senior vice president of engineering, and Tom and Rich Cerilli for their introductions to published authors from whose experiences I could learn.

My son for advising against an earlier, inferior book title, elder daughter for sharing her college job-seeking experiences, and all three of my children for reminding me what it's like for young adults and teens to begin making their way in the world.

Kevin Collins, Catherine Copetas, Eden Fisher, Jonathan Kersting, Mary McKinney, Dana Pless, and Melissa Ungar for their speaking and writing invitations which helped me clarify the ideas.

Daniel Rosati for suggesting a key reason why people fail to seek advice, which I hadn't thought of.

Bonnie Granat for her insightful editing of the manuscript.

Andrea Gondi for her creative and flexible book cover design.

Professors Jeswald Salacuse, Yulia Chentsova, Christine Whelan, Jessica Wolfendale, Lori Foster Thompson, Heejung Kim, and Fred Bryant for reprints and help with relevant insights from academic research.

Names connected with real-life stories are fictitious, except for my own.

My Vivisimo co-founders Christopher Palmer and Jerome Pesenti enabled the rich company-building experiences that imbue this book. My Carnegie Mellon graduate-school advisor, the late Herbert A. Simon, taught me how to think and write clearly; any remaining obscurity is because I wouldn't let him finish the job. My Philosophy teacher, Adolf Grunbaum of the University of Pittsburgh, taught all his students how good-looking arguments often turn ugly upon skillful inspection.

Finally, my father and mother taught me the right ways to do things by their example. My wife Carmen encouraged the many evenings of research and writing that led to this book.

Table of Contents

Part I - The Landscape
1. People Often Don't Seek Advice, but Should
2. What Advice Does for You
3. 28 Reasons for not Seeking Advice

Part II - Scouting Reports
4. What Advice Books Say
5. What Research Says
6. What Proverbs Say

Part III - The Map
7. When You Should Seek Advice
8. Who is a Good Advisor
9. How to Get an Advisor
10. How to Set Up an Advice Process
11. Dealing with Contradictory Advice

Part IV - Boulders and Watering Holes
12. The Role of the Web and Social Media
13. Advice as a Rule, not an Exception
14. A Peek at an Advice-Centric Environment
15. Advice Seeking in Different Cultures

Part V - Paths Well Traveled
16. What Major Should I Study?
17. Should I Change Jobs?
18. Should I Hire this Person?

Part VI - The Destination
19. Get Advice and Prosper

CHAPTERS

Chapter 1: People Don't Seek Advice, but Should 11

Chapter 2: What Advice Does for You 17

Chapter 3: Twenty-Eight Reasons for Not Seeking Advice............................27

Chapter 4: What Advice Books Say..47

Chapter 5: What Research Says...61

Chapter 6: What Proverbs Say 71

Chapter 7: When You Should Seek Advice 83

Chapter 8: Who is a Good Advisor?...93

Chapter 9: How to Get an Advisor...101

Chapter 10: How to Set Up an Advice Process.....................................111

Chapter 11: Dealing with Contradictory Advice...................................123

Chapter 12: The Role of the Web and Social Media...............................129

Chapter 13: Advice as a Rule, not an Exception 139

Chapter 14: A Peek at an Advice-Centric Environment.................................143

Chapter 15: Advice Seeking in Different Cultures 153

Chapter 16: What Major Should I Study?...157

Chapter 17: Should I Change Jobs?..165

Chapter 18: Should I Hire this Person? 171

Chapter 19: Get Advice and Prosper 179

Chapter 1: People Often Don't Seek Advice, but Should

In the late 1970s I was an undergraduate studying engineering at the University of Illinois at Chicago, then known as Chicago Circle. In those days, Chicago Circle was a relatively new branch campus of the University of Illinois, in the shadow of the older, larger, and more prestigious campus at Urbana-Champaign. "Circle" was an undistinguished commuter campus with no dorms in which 90% of the students were the first in their family to graduate from college. Circle gave its students a low-cost, good-quality education within a compact campus easily accessible from the subway. Circle today has grown beyond its humble origins into a major research campus and medical school.

At Circle I became friends with Conrad (not his real name), an engineering classmate who had a full scholarship from his home country, which was investing some of its windfall oil revenues in a foundation that sent bright students to study abroad. Conrad had all expenses paid to wherever he could get accepted in the United States. Since Conrad wanted to study electronics engineering, he consulted the information available to him where he lived—a large city that was home to his country's oil industry—and opted to apply to the only two universities in the United States that he mistakenly believed offered electronics engineering: the University of Illinois at Chicago Circle and another school in Louisiana.

I was amazed when Conrad told me his story and said that he had not really consulted anyone in making his college application decisions. So a bright student with a prestigious all-expenses-paid scholarship to anywhere in the United States ended up attending Chicago Circle when he could have been admitted to any number of better-regarded schools at the time. If Conrad had consulted an electrical engineer, or likely any engineer in his home city, he probably would have been told something like this: "Don't be silly! Electronics engineering is just a new subfield of electrical engineering, so you have many dozens of targets, not just two! Apply to electrical engineering departments!" (As a newer campus, Chicago Circle had adopted modernistic, non-traditional names for its engineering majors.) Conrad could have told his parents, a family friend, or even his foundation sponsor, "I'm thinking of applying to these two schools to study electronics engineering. Please find me an engineer to talk with so I can get some advice." But he didn't. As I recall, he didn't because it just *didn't occur to him.* Now I'm sure that Conrad has done well in the years since our days at Circle, but that doesn't change the fact that Conrad made a faulty choice based on a faulty process.

I've kept this story in mind for many years, although it didn't prevent me from making similar youthful mistakes, and I have collected many similar stories that involve me or others as protagonist. In most of these situations, a course of action was called for, and usually the person who made the decision did not seek advice from others. The outcomes were sometimes unsatisfactory and other times satisfactory but likely inferior to other outcomes that, had we been armed with knowledgeable advice from others and the confidence that it instills, were within reach.

Human beings have a prodigious capacity to learn from peers, not just from those who raised us as children. People make use of the knowledge of others by reading books. Scientists stand on the shoulders of giants—to use the celebrated phrase of the 17th-century scientist Sir Isaac Newton—by studying the research articles of their hundreds or even hundreds of thousands of scientific peers. Today, Internet users consult the Web for everything from consumer purchasing decisions to advice on vacation destinations and removing viruses from one's computer. However, on highly individual issues that are not suited for mass-audience books and the Internet, our uniquely human capacity to learn from others via face-to-face dialogue and consultation is much underused.

During the decades since I learned Conrad's story, I have come to realize, through reflection as well as practice, that it's possible for everyone to do better in their personal and working lives. It's possible to become more knowledgeable, even expert, at the crucial skill of seeking advice by acknowledging and building upon a couple of obvious truths:

- No matter how knowledgeable, smart, or experienced you are about an issue, someone else is more knowledgeable, smarter, or more experienced than you, with few exceptions! And that person may even be down the hall from you.

- Even if you know a thousand things, consulting someone who knows only a hundred will teach you something you didn't know, since the overlap isn't perfect. Two heads are better than one, according to folk wisdom.

During their upbringing, children are trained to give thanks when receiving a favor and to excuse themselves when causing a bother or injury. However, adolescents are rarely trained, when facing a problem, to ask themselves if they have the knowledge needed to address the problem and, if not, who does and can help. Instead, they tend to *go it alone* and learn to seek advice only gradually, over many years if at all. Going it alone tends to bring about inferior decisions both at work and in life generally.

In brief, my message is that *winners* make better decisions by seeking out advice, advice is *not* for pipsqueaks and losers, and everyone—including this author—can get better at seeking advice. With this book, I hope to encourage a cultural shift in which *expertise* in seeking advice is itself sought and celebrated.

How does advice seeking differ from personal networking, the subject of popular business books? Advice seeking is *problem-driven*—motivated by specific problems or issues—whereas networking is activity-*driven*—motivated by the desire to enlarge one's circle of acquaintances in anticipation of some future need. The best networker in the world might not actively seek advice, much less be skilled at it. Conversely, a skilled advice seeker need not have many acquaintances, although this definitely helps. The bottom line is that reading the world's best how-to networking book won't help you become a better advice seeker, and the subjects discussed in this book are not suitable for a book on networking.

What justifies an author's hope that he can bring into the world insights that are not already expressed in the millions of books that have been published? I aim to combine the following circumstances and experiences:

- A long-standing wonder at why people often don't seek advice, since I enjoy doing it and consider doing it well to be a worthwhile and interesting challenge that leads to better decisions and outcomes.

- The good fortune of having studied, worked, or taught in several countries as a young adult (Spain, Brazil, and China) where everything was new and sometimes bewildering, and calling on others for help was essential in order for me to thrive—or even survive.

- Later, as an academic researcher, my goal was to understand the knowledge that is needed to carry out certain intellectual tasks and to try to "put structure" on them: make the tasks more systematic and recipe-like, possibly leading to computer programs that could do the tasks automatically for people or assist them. Perhaps this background in task analysis can be applied to the social, emotional, and intellectual challenge of advice seeking.

- As an entrepreneur who co-founded and led a software company with two other computer scientists who knew no more about business than I did, I faced the challenge of learning quickly about all aspects of the technology business. Books, articles, and the Web were valuable, but they were not enough. I needed to explain our own company's circumstances to someone and get targeted advice, and I needed to do so without embarrassment as a 43-year-old who society, at that age, often expected to have all the answers, or at least to pretend that he had them.

- The company I co-founded—Vivisimo, acquired in 2012 by IBM—is in the business of helping users find and leverage information. Along with my CEO duties, I worked for years on how people could best leverage information through search engines for their personal and work activities.

- Finally, through my own children, I've reacquainted myself with the challenges that youth face in making their way in the world and with their frequent reluctance to learn from others' experience. This youthful attitude is just like the one that Conrad, I, and many others of my acquaintance have had toward seeking advice.

Putting these circumstances and experiences together, I offer this book as a brief but comprehensive look at a neglected area: advice seeking in work and personal life. Many prominent self-help books, such as *The 7 Habits of Highly Effective People*, have tended to deal with character development of the whole human being, his or her relationships with others, and behaviors that lead to fulfillment and happiness. I have no such ambition. Instead, I write for readers who may or may not be fulfilled and happy but who can benefit from improving along just one dimension, although it's a dimension with a potentially broad effect on people's lives. Attentive readers should, if I have succeeded, become both more proactive in seeking advice and more skilled at it, which will have a positive impact on their overall effectiveness. Proactive advice seeking is a skill that is gradually acquired over a lifetime. If I can accelerate this by years or even decades by having written this book, we are all winners.

On problems that can benefit from careful thought, the principles and methods set forth in this book will help you do the following:

- *Think of* getting advice.

- Decide if seeking it is worthwhile in this case.

- Figure out who are good advisors.

- Do background research.

- Approach advisors productively.

- Engage with them in human terms.

- Evaluate their counsel.

- Choose the best courses of action with more confidence.

- *Not* agonize every step of the way.

This book unfolds with a traveler's metaphor. We'll continue surveying the *landscape* by explaining in detail how advice can help (it's not just for solutions!). Then we'll describe the many flawed reasons that lead people not to seek advice, ranging from the failure of imagination to pragmatic, cultural, emotional, and even biological factors.

Next, we'll get *scouting reports* from scholarly research articles, folk and expert wisdom through proverbs and quotations as well as through previous books on self-help, advice, and self-reliance. Let's build on what our predecessors have already achieved.

The how-to part of the book is the **map**: judging when to get advice, the characteristics of good advisors, how to identify, approach, prepare for, meet, and follow up with them, and how to deal with contradictory advice.

There are *boulders and watering holes* along the way, though. You'll want to leverage the Web but not rely on it exclusively, learn how to make advice seeking a habit, and understand how advice fits in with various cultures, from advice-intensive cultures like scientific research to national cultures unlike that of the United States.

Your journey may come across some *paths well traveled*. The individual characteristics of these paths—picking a college major, changing jobs, and recruiting and hiring employees—justify saying a bit more about them.

Having arrived at our *destination*, we'll notice new productive and fulfilling paths to follow that would have stayed unseen if we had jetted to the destination, unaware of the rich terrain below, instead of hiking and taking it all in.

Chapter 2: What Advice Does for You

What does advice consist of and what do people gain from it—what are its benefits? People clearly want solutions to their problems, but that's not all they should want or expect. This chapter sets up a framework that will help interpret what others have written about advice and will provide our later how-to chapters with the right structure so that advice seeking can become more predictable and fruitful. But first, let's consider a prominent example of seeking advice.

Dale Carnegie in his classic *How to Win Friends and Influence People* tells a story about President Abraham Lincoln's deliberations on a proclamation to free the slaves.

> During the darkest hours of the Civil War, Lincoln wrote to an old friend in Springfield, Illinois, asking him to come to Washington. Lincoln said he had some problems he wanted to discuss with him. The old neighbor called at the White House, and Lincoln talked to him for hours about the advisability of issuing a proclamation freeing the slaves. Lincoln went over all the arguments for and against such a move, and then read letters and newspaper articles, some denouncing him for not freeing the slaves and others denouncing him for fear he was going to free them. After talking for hours, Lincoln shook hands with his old

> neighbor, said good night, and sent him back to Illinois
> without even asking for his opinion. Lincoln had done all the
> talking himself. That seemed to clarify his mind. "He seemed
> to feel easier after that talk," the old friend said. Lincoln
> hadn't wanted advice. He had wanted merely a friendly,
> sympathetic listener to whom he could unburden himself.

It's remarkable that Lincoln discussed the "advisability" of issuing a proclamation but never asked his old friend for his opinion nor "wanted advice," according to his friend. I interpret this to mean that Lincoln didn't ask his old friend to recommend a solution to his problem: whether or not to proclaim emancipation of the slaves. So did Lincoln seek advice, or did he not? Our answer to this is a clear "yes," which the remainder of this chapter will explain.

Research Findings

In order to set up a framework of what advice does for you—its benefits—I reviewed the scholarly literature for its insights. Later chapters will also review and build upon what scholars have learned about the advisory process, but here we look at some basic ideas in that literature in order to devise our framework.

S. Bonaccio and R. S. Dalal, in a 2006 article ("Advice Taking and Decision Making: An Integrative Literature Review, and Implications for the Organizational Sciences") in the journal *Organizational Behavior and Human Decision Processes*, stated:

> Decision-makers seek out and attend to advice in order to
> share accountability for the outcome of the decision and to
> improve the probability that their decisions will be accurate
> or optimal ... For instance, interacting with others prior to
> making a decision forces decision-makers to think of the
> decision problem in new ways ... and provides decision-
> makers with new information or alternatives not previously
> considered ...
> ... input from others was sought because it could help
> decision-makers make better decisions and avoid mistakes,
> help them think about new information, help them organize

18

> their thoughts, and help them become more confident in
> their decisions. Furthermore, advice could include the
> provision of social support needed for the decision.

From this we can enumerate four ways that advice helps us: in making better decisions, in feeling more confident, in sharing accountability, and in gaining ongoing support. The first one— in making better decisions—is this book's main focus, but let's take a look at the other three.

Advice can boost the advice seeker's **confidence**, especially for courses of action that don't result in a clear-cut win/lose outcome. Lacking confidence, the advice seeker may not follow up with the needed conviction and energy, or he may be plagued with remorseful self-doubt about the decision process or the decision itself. The advice seeker needs an answer to the following question: "Am I missing something?" Once the decision is made, it's not good to be forever questioning oneself.

Advice can enable **shared accountability** when others share the responsibility for the outcome, also known as "covering your a__ (or your backside)" or spreading the blame. More positively, if the action requires **ongoing support** from others, then seeking their contributions in the form of advice will commit them emotionally to the undertaking because they feel a part of it from the start. J. W. Salacuse writes in his book *The Wise Advisor* that "a person may ask the advice of another as a tactic to influence the advisor. It is always flattering to be asked for advice."

Five Benefits

Now let's set up the detailed framework of the benefits of advice, borrowing from scholarly research. In a 2001 article ("Beyond Answers: Dimensions of the Advice Network") in the journal *Social Networks*, authors R. Cross, S. P. Borgatti, and A. Parker studied the advice that consultants in a consulting firm got from their social networks and identified the following five types of advice:

1. **Solutions**—An advisor provides information that is used to generate solutions to problems, especially how-to information.
2. **Pointers**—An advisor gives pointers to individuals, locations, or documents that have relevant expertise. (The cited article calls this "meta-knowledge.")

3. **Framing**—The advisor points out aspects of the problem that may not be recognized, helping to change how one frames the problem and the criteria that a solution should meet. The advisor can also point out how various courses of action could go wrong. (The cited article calls this "problem reformulation").
4. **Validation**—An advisor provides confidence that one's approach or solution is a good one.
5. **Legitimation**—A respected advisor becomes a source of credibility that helps one move toward a solution.

I'll illustrate these five types of advice with a fictional but representative case: Daisy, a recent college graduate who majored in liberal arts, is seeking advice on how to find a job. Daisy started out by replying to want ads and electronic job postings but has had little luck in even getting interviews. Daisy has visited many websites in her search for guidance but is bewildered by the variety of recommendations, and she questions whether all the information she's found applies to her circumstances. Maybe Daisy has even read the Prologue to Herman Hesse's *Demian* in her literature classes, which teaches that "... every man is more than just himself; he also represents the unique, the very special and always significant and remarkable point at which the world's phenomena intersect, only once in this way and never again."

1. **Solutions**—An advisor provides information that is used to generate solutions to problems, especially how-to information.

Although there is plenty of job-seeking advice in books and on the Web, Daisy has not yet realized that most jobs are found not by responding to job postings but by people-to-people contact, also known as networking. This is especially true of a liberal-arts graduate, indeed of most college majors except for the minority for whom it's clear what type of job they will be slotted for at least initially: Engineering majors will work as engineers, nursing majors as nurses, computer science majors as programmers, plumbing majors as plumbers, and education majors as teachers. Even, for example, a biology, chemistry, or physics major does not know what type of work to do, since jobs as biologists, chemists, and physicists typically require advanced degrees. Daisy hasn't realized this, partly because her best friend is a nursing student and her elder brother, with whom she is close, was an engineering student, and they had no problems finding where to apply or getting job offers.

After listening to Daisy's short-term and longer-term goals and her attempts so far, the advisor may suggest that Daisy contact recent graduates

20

she may have met and known as a freshman or sophomore but who graduated and are now working. She would then ask them for their suggestions or any inside knowledge of job openings that they could share with her. The advisor may even suggest types of job or locales that Daisy hasn't considered. Daisy may also be urged to set the goal of contacting a new person every day, meeting face-to-face whenever possible, explaining to them her circumstances and goals, and asking for their suggestions or knowledge of openings.

Of course, the simplest way to provide advice of this type is to directly offer Daisy a solution in the form of a job, or to introduce her to someone who has need of an entry-level college graduate with her profile.

2. **Pointers**—An advisor gives pointers to individuals, locations, or documents that have relevant expertise. (The cited article calls this "meta-knowledge.")

Fellow alumni are a good source of help in finding internships or jobs. Daisy may not have thought of this, so the advisor suggests meeting with a career counselor at her college, and contacting the alumni club, if there is one, at the locale where Daisy is looking for a job.

It also turns out that Daisy was an active member of a college sorority, so her advisor points out that a professional networking site like LinkedIn can be a good source of leads. Daisy is instructed to search LinkedIn for members who list that sorority, are employed in her targeted geographic area, and are fellow alumnae of her college. Her searches turn up a dozen matches, some of whom are likely to offer suggestions as fellow alums and sorority sisters.

3. **Framing**—The advisor points out aspects of the problem that may not yet be recognized, helping to change how one frames the problem and the criteria that a solution should meet.

Daisy may view her problem as finding a job. However, finding a job is really a means to an end, but maybe other means can achieve the same end. Daisy may just be doing what is expected and "normal." The advisor talks with Daisy to find out what her ends really are, while being aware that she may not really know and shouldn't be made to feel bad if she doesn't know. Here are some possible ends:

*   Make money and support herself, or help support others.
*   Advance in her career.

21

- Have fun.
- See the world. For example, live abroad, which may be difficult later.
- Save the world. That is, act on her idealism.
- Serve her country, her faith, or other grouping.
- A combination of the above.

Daisy might be helped, although she might just be confused, by a dialogue along these lines, which can help frame her problem less as "finding a job" and instead as "What do I do next, within my possibilities?" Thus, Daisy might decide that she doesn't have a critical need for money (she needs to support nobody but herself, and partially at that), but she does want to learn as much as she can and have varied task experience, right out of the college gate. In that case, she might start looking for a job in small companies, where she can learn to perform many tasks, or she might prioritize her job search according to the qualities of her employer or her direct supervisor. In other words: Don't find a job, find a boss.

4. **Validation**—An advisor provides confidence that one's approach or solution is a good one.

Although she doesn't know how to find a job, maybe Daisy has figured out that she wants to attend law school after working for a few years. She has heard that working as a paralegal is a good way to see what lawyers do before making a career and dollar investment in law school but is unsure if she should instead try to find a job that pays more. The advisor, after listening to her financial circumstances (for example, she can live at home and not pay rent), may validate that her goal makes sense. Encouraged by this, Daisy goes on job interviews exuding a newfound confidence in her career goal, which appeals to her interviewers.

On the other hand, Daisy may have lived all her life in Podunk, USA, and may be eager to see the world (or wants to see Podunk after only breathing Manhattan air) before accumulating responsibilities, career progression, and even family of her own. None of her friends shares this eagerness, so she might feel selfish or weird, and so seeks advice in the form of encouragement that it's not so weird and selfish. The advisor might be able to point out examples of peers who did the same and arrange for a phone call in which Daisy can hear about others' experiences.

5. **Legitimation**—A respected advisor becomes a source of credibility that helps move toward a solution.

As Daisy encounters difficulty in finding a job after graduation, she turns to an impartial family friend or to Uncle Damon for advice on what to do. Encouraged by her loving parents, who have always lived in their hometown, Daisy focuses her job search locally but wonders if that's the best way to leverage her costly four years of college study. Uncle Damon listens to her thoughts and desires, quizzes Daisy on her relationship to her parents and their wishes, and then recommends that she expand her search to other towns in the state using her still-fresh contacts gained while she served on the Student Senate. Bolstered by Uncle Damon's support, she discusses the idea with her parents, who agree that Daisy should expand her geographic focus.

The cited authors' main finding was that "managers do use different people for different things, but that this is based on a kind of ranking ... in which some contacts are used for everything, while others are used for 'intermediate' things, and still others are only used for 'simple' things." So advisors who provide high-end legitimation also tend to be able to offer solutions, pointers, framing, and validation. Thus, for example, a classmate of your same age may point you to a job opening as an elementary form of advice but not be able to help you conceive of the problem differently or to legitimate or validate your options.

A Sixth Benefit: Social Engagement

I believe, however, that the scholarly authors miss one benefit of advice seeking that will become the sixth benefit in our completed framework—engagement. Engagement helps build social capital, which sociologists such as R. D. Putnam in his book *Bowling Alone: The Collapse and Revival of American Community* characterizes as follows:

> Civic engagement and social capital entail mutual obligation and responsibility for action. [...] Your extended family represents a form of social capital, as do your Sunday school class, the regulars who play poker on your commuter train, your college roommates, the civic organization to which you belong, the Internet chat group in which you participate, and the network of professional acquaintances recorded in your address book.

Let's now list all the six benefits that advice can bring:

23

1. **Solutions**—An advisor provides information that is used to generate solutions to problems, especially how-to information.
2. **Pointers**—An advisor gives pointers to individuals, locations, or documents that have relevant expertise. (The cited article calls this "meta-knowledge.")
3. **Framing**—The advisor points out aspects of the problem that may not be recognized, helping to change how one frames the problem and the criteria that a solution should meet.
4. **Validation**—An advisor provides confidence that one's approach or solution is a good one.
5. **Legitimation**—A respected advisor becomes a source of credibility that helps one move toward a solution.
6. **Engagement**—An agreeable (pleasurable) experience that provides memorable moments and may help build social capital.

Daisy may deepen her relationship with Uncle Damon by consulting him on her career moves. Daisy might also engage with her friends, from whom she doesn't expect much in the form of useful advice or support but rather collegial engagement that builds social capital.

Elsewhere in this book I tell the story of stopping in northern Indiana and consulting with a state park officer about the best places to go to have my prepared dinner on a Lake Michigan beach, pausing from my long drive to Chicago and trying to avoid Chicago's evening rush hour. The officer kindly pointed me to the beach that the locals access for free rather than the state park, which would have cost $10 to park my car in. Although I did not build useful social capital with the Indiana officer, whom I'll never come across again, I did appreciate his advice, which made me feel good about his state, and it provided a memorable human moment that I remember as much as the visuals of the Indiana lakefront, sand, and fellow beachgoers, and more than my nondescript dinner.

Let's wrap up the message of this chapter: Advice can offer solutions, pointers, framing, validation, legitimation, and engagement, all in the service of making better decisions that are more likely to help one achieve one's goal and of building human relationships. The detailed framework of five concrete benefits borrowed from scholarly research, plus one additional benefit with a social dimension, should lead the reader to realize the following:

1. Advice does not consist only of solutions. If someone offers counsel but confesses upfront that he doesn't have a solution (for example, a job for job-seekers), don't spurn the offer.

2. Others won't think you are weak or scatterbrained if what you need is more than just recommended "solutions." If they do, then they likely are poor advisors anyway.

3. The best advisors may be able to help on all the levels of the framework. Treasure them.

4. Consider asking targeted questions within one of the levels. For example: What aspects of the problem am I not seeing? Or, I'm inclined to evaluate the options along these dimensions—what other dimensions should I consider?

This chapter has surveyed the landscape of advice seeking by analyzing in detail what is to be gained by completing the journey. The next chapter will examine the diverse reasons why people often don't make the trip, reasons that include intellectual (flawed knowledge, judgment, and reasoning), emotional, social, and even biological factors.

Chapter 3: 28 Reasons for Not Seeking Advice

The first two chapters made the case for why advice is important and discussed its various benefits, which go far beyond merely recommending solutions to problems. Later chapters will provide guidance on identifying advisors, recognizing suitable ones, approaching them, getting their advice, and establishing good relations. Impatient readers may jump to those chapters, but my recommendation is to invest first in a greater understanding of the advisory process from different angles. This chapter looks at the many reasons why people fail to seek advice; you might recognize yourself or others in these reasons.

A truism is that men don't ask for directions. Nowadays, fewer people need to ask for driving directions because of car-mounted GPS, driving-directions websites like Mapquest and Google Maps, and sophisticated mobile devices. But is this truism true? As reported by Scott Mayerowitz of ABC News in late 2010, research by the British auto insurance company Sheila's Wheels revealed that British men indeed ask for directions less often than do women, leading annually to an extra 276 miles of driving while lost, versus a smaller amount for women. Moreover, the report also stated that "more than one out of four men—26 percent—wait at least half an hour before asking for directions, with a stubborn 12 percent refusing to ask a stranger for help at all." As far as I can recall, my own late father, God bless him, never once asked for driving directions in my presence as a passenger. Personally, I have never understood this. A lost motorist drives around looking for a destination while surrounded by pedestrians who are experts at finding it, most of whom would be happy to share their knowledge, yet the motorist won't make the consultation. How absurd and ineffective.

As mentioned previously, as an undergraduate in the late 1970s, I studied computer engineering at the University of Illinois at Chicago, known as Chicago Circle in those days. UICC was a commuter campus of little distinction at the time. I had good grades and wasn't quite ready to join the workforce, so I opted to apply to master's programs. Without seeking input from anyone, I decided to apply to three graduate schools: MIT, Caltech, and my same department. In those days, college applications were more burdensome than today, since everything was done on paper rather than online, and in particular the MIT application demanded to know every course you ever took as well as the textbook used in each course. Regardless, applying to only the top two schools in the country, plus the safe choice of my alma mater, was a mistake, since I had nothing going for me except grades. The right course obviously would have been to apply to some of the second-tier, but still very competitive, departments. Predictably (in hindsight), MIT and Caltech both rejected me, so I completed my master's at UICC. I learned a lot and my life turned out fine, but still the process was mistaken.

Why didn't I seek input from anybody? Certainly there were graduate students who had been teaching assistants in my classes and professors whose courses I had done well in. I didn't seek input because ... *it didn't occur to me!* How easy it would have been to just approach a grad student or professor and say, "I would like to get a master's and am thinking of applying to these schools. Could I get your input? What do you think?" Since I didn't have a honed skill of anticipating future scenarios and adjusting my approach based on that analysis, I took an easy, simple step and that was that.

Let's take another example, after years had passed and my outlook on advice had evolved. During the early days of Vivisimo, the software company I co-founded in 2000 with two young computer scientists, Jerome Pesenti and Christopher Palmer, at Carnegie Mellon University, I occasionally went on business trips with Jerome. He had a very different travel approach than I did, leading to some humorous disagreements. Jerome had a background in orienteering, a sport that originated in Scandinavia that involves racing across unfamiliar terrain with map and compass toward a specific destination. Needless to say, orienteering doesn't allow competitors to stop to ask for directions! Often I would be driving, wanting to stop the car to consult a local, whereas Jerome would want to use his orienteering approach to figure it out on the fly. Actually, either method worked, thanks to Jerome's skill and quick thinking. The larger question is whether the orienteering approach serves as the right mind-set for life's other challenges.

A final poignant example comes from a personal blog entry entitled, "On the importance of mentors," which I came across while looking up someone's background on the Web after an acquaintance had made an introduction:

> I grew up assuming that people make their own way in the world. I thought it was up to me to make every decision, plan every move, open every door, and find my own way in my life and career. Only much later did I learn that I was doing it all wrong. Not only is my way much harder, it's also completely miserable to be so isolated. Here's an example. The place where I started making these wrong decisions was in college.

The 28 Reasons

I have come to believe that people fail to seek advice for many different reasons. I created the following list of 28 reasons after reflecting on my own life experiences, my readings and observations, and numerous discussions with others who pointed out reasons that had escaped me. Since 28 items of anything are too many to comprehend without grouping them, I've put them into four categories:

- Intellectual—Having to do with the logic of the circumstances, the goals, and the advisor recommendations.

- Emotional—Involving inner-directed emotions of the advice seeker.

- Social—Relating to advisory interactions or the emotions of advisors.

- Biological—Factors that are biological or societal in origin.

First let's list the 28 reasons.

Intellectual Reasons

1. It just doesn't occur to them to seek advice.

2. They're unsure how to go about it.

3. They may end up with more questions than they started with.

4. They've gotten contradictory advice in the past and are unsure how to deal with it.

5. Young people, in particular, may fall prey to the dynamic of undervaluing the counsel of older people or thinking that times have changed so their elders' experience no longer applies.

6. They think a subject or circumstance is so unprecedented that no advice seems worthwhile.

7. The issue doesn't seem important or difficult enough to go to the trouble of seeking advice.

8. A viable option is to do nothing, even if it's not the best option, so they neither seek advice on positive actions nor take any positive actions even without seeking advice, due to the comfort of inertia.

9. A low level of knowledge—whether in general or specific to the problem—causes people to "not know what they don't know" and fail to recognize that they have a knowledge or experience gap.

10. The tremendous amount of information and opinion on the Web, as well as the rise of social media, leads people to think that those are good enough sources of guidance.

Emotional Reasons

11. They believe that seeking advice shows weakness.

12. They just want the freedom to make their own mistakes.

13. By temperament, they prefer to take action rather than to reflect and think things through.

14. The courses of action lead to a clear-cut success or failure, which would become known to others if advice were sought.

15. They avoid reaching out because of shyness, not for any practical or intellectual reasons.

16. The situation involves confidential or embarrassing details that people prefer not to share, because word could spread beyond the advisor, and even discussing the issue only with an advisor is discomfiting enough.

17. People like to display consistency, so they persist alone in a failed situation in order to avoid publicly changing course.

18. Their minds are already made up, so they avoid asking for advice for fear that others would contradict their decision.

19. They fear that involving an advisor may lead to a loss of control that could spiral into an undesirable outcome.

20. Their school training led them to attempt (homework) problems by themselves before seeking help, so they carry over that learned behavior to real-life problems, which unlike homework are not done as practice for a test!

Social Reasons

21. They believe that others dislike giving advice and thus are reluctant to ask.

22. They don't want to impose on others' time or goodwill.

23. They don't know whom to ask.

24. Nobody else seems knowledgeable about their situation.

25. They avoid consulting others in authority over them, such as a workplace superior or their parents, because they don't want to feel obligated to follow their advice or risk causing offense.

26. They may not want to share credit with others for their subsequent accomplishments.

Biological Reasons

27. Cultural factors, particularly for those in the United States who came from other countries, may discourage advice seeking for varying reasons.

28. Biological research reveals that adolescents, unlike children and adults, are risk-prone, and that certain genes predispose some people to seek social support and others to avoid it.

Next, as we go through each of those reasons, ask yourself if you see a resemblance to mistakes in your past, or in the present of others close to you, or if any of these reasons prevent you from building on others' expertise today.

Intellectual Reasons

1. It just doesn't occur to them to seek advice.

People are "trained" to seek advice in conventional situations. On health issues, see a doctor. For legal issues, consult an attorney. Contact a real estate agent to help you become familiar with the local neighborhoods before moving to a new area. It's no coincidence that these situations correspond to specific professions, and if there's enough demand, then new paid professions arise, such as college counselors or college-planning consultants. But for many of life's issues that don't bring to mind paying a professional, seeking informal advice proactively just doesn't occur to people. Sometimes people don't even realize that there are aspects of the situation that they might not be seeing, so they don't look deeper. Or maybe they've never before asked anyone for general advice, as opposed to, say, specific help on a homework problem, so they have to "discover" that it can be done. They are virginal advice seekers.

2. They're unsure how to go about it.

Advice seeking is acquired like any other skill. Nobody is born with it, everyone has to do it for the first time, some people do it better than others for a variety of reasons, and repetition improves performance, especially when combined with learning from cases that went awry. Finally, it is a skill that can be *taught*. It would help if people, especially young people, were shown very simple ways to ask for advice, and this will be dealt with in later chapters.

3. They may end up with more questions than they started with.

A truly expert advice giver, realizing that the details of the situation matter, should understand the seeker's particular circumstances, so it may be necessary to ask questions that the seeker hasn't thought about. Let's consider my own experience in applying to graduate school just out of college, when I didn't seek any advice and followed a mistaken approach. To fully understand my circumstances, an advice giver might have asked me the following:

- Why do you want to go to graduate school?
- Are you sure that you want to do a master's in computer engineering?
- Do you want to stop after a master's, or is it possible you may want to do a Ph.D.?
- How much financial aid do you need?
- What factors are important to you? Geography, proximity to family, weather, prospects of finding a job in the same location, etc.?
- What would you like to do after graduate school?
- What would you like to do with your life?

The quality of the advice provided increases along with the amount that the advice giver knows about the advice seeker, but such a situation can be uncomfortable for them both if the latter, especially younger ones, do not know the answer to most of these questions.

One of my daughters tells me of visiting the career services office at her college during her freshman year in search of a summer internship. The career services counselor began by asking many questions: "What do you want to major in? Where do you want to live? What do you want to do after you graduate?" Discouraged by not knowing the answers and maybe even looking foolish, she lost interest in seeking help from the office and found a summer job by other means—someone told her about a specific concrete opportunity and confirmed her interest in applying. My daughter says that it would have been more effective had the interviewer shown her some examples and said: "A number of other students with your background and interests worked at these jobs and enjoyed them; do any of them appeal to you?"

The overall point is that people may be discouraged from seeking advice because they anticipate having to deal with too many preliminary questions whose answers they don't know. A skillful advice giver is sensitive to this and adjusts the approach, or an expert advice seeker may coach the advice giver as to what type of advice is best offered. Thus, my daughter could have coached the career services counselor. Rather than saying, "I'm looking for a summer internship" and then responding to the questions of the counselor, she could instead have started with or replied that she was "interested in a summer internship, don't have fixed ideas, have broad interests, and am looking for something that has been interesting for freshmen like me in the past." Someone capable of thus structuring the session shows real skill in advice seeking, but nobody can be expected to possess such skill without substantial life experience or training. This book offers that training.

4. They've gotten contradictory advice in the past and are unsure how to deal with it.

Weighing multiple pieces of advice is a difficult task, especially because the advice may be contradictory in details or in the overall recommendation.

For example, in my nine years as CEO of Vivisimo, one key decision impelled me to systematically seek advice, which came out all over the map. Vivisimo was a largely bootstrapped software company, which means that it grew mostly by reinvesting its own revenue rather than by capital from investors. (The exceptions were the very early days when we relied on federal Small Business Innovation Research grants from the National Science Foundation and long-term loans from the Commonwealth of Pennsylvania's Ben Franklin program, which through its Pittsburgh affiliate Innovation Works made small investments in technology companies.)

After seven years, we had a solid product and customer base and employed about 60 people. We had identified a large market where we were defeating much larger companies in competitive situations. These circumstances led us to seek outside risk capital to grow the company faster than what our own revenue from customers would enable. Apart from federal research grants and state-sponsored loans, I had never raised capital from professional investors. There were three options:

- Raise the capital by myself.
- Hire a professional agent or banker to raise the capital and pay a fee upon success.
- Hire a Chief Financial Officer (CFO) who had done it before, working closely with that CFO but letting him or her lead the charge.

I visited three accomplished business leaders whom I knew: the ex-CEO of a small, local public company, the founder/CEO of a small software company, and the head of a nonprofit that promoted the development of technology companies and was himself a former CEO. Each of these three advisors gave me a recommendation for a different option! If my memory serves, their rationales were:

- **Raise capital by myself.** Potential investors would think there was something wrong with me if I wasn't able to do it myself.

- **Hire a professional agent.** This advisor had had success with outside agents, and was also able to personally recommend a good one.

- **Hire a Chief Financial Officer.** Rely on someone who had done it before, or it would be too large a task to undertake at the same time one is running the company as CEO.

I was puzzled at first by the incompatible pieces of advice. But then I recalled something my old graduate school advisor liked to point out: Folk knowledge comes in contradictory pairs, so the Devil (or God) is in the details. For example: "Haste makes waste" and "slow and steady wins the race", versus "Don't leave for tomorrow what you can do today" and "the early bird gets the worm." Or "Two's company and three's a crowd" versus "the more the merrier." It should have been no surprise to me that expert knowledge could come not only in contradictory pairs, but in contradictory triplets!

I resolved the contradiction by deciding to recruit a CFO, because I didn't relish raising capital by myself, and the lack of a long-standing relationship with an agent or banker made me uncomfortable in going that route, given the high stakes. A wrong course could have been very damaging to our small company of about 60 people whose livelihoods depended on choosing well. I had to reconcile what felt right for me with what made general sense. As it turned out, the recruited CFO and I raised capital for Vivisimo successfully, and I think it was absolutely the right decision, pursued confidently. Confidence came not only from the recommendation itself but from knowing that I had heard and considered other options that I rejected based on reasons I could articulate.

Did this need to choose among completely different recommendations discourage me from seeking advice again on similar issues? Not as far as I can tell. It does help to be comfortable with ambiguity and uncertainty as well as to know in advance that receiving conflicting advice is not unusual.

5. **Young people, in particular, may fall prey to the dynamic of undervaluing the counsel of older people or thinking that times have changed so their elders' experience no longer applies.**

Everyone knows that young people don't listen to elders, or at least not to their parents. Maybe trailblazing is part of every human's biological makeup. Youth often feel that elders don't understand the world as it is today, or that circumstances are so different that advice from elders is worthless. Since young people especially have underdeveloped skill or experience in seeking advice, this means that they consult nobody, except maybe peers who are inexperienced both in worldly matters and in advice giving itself. Is this unavoidable or can it be fixed?

In my parents' native tongue (Spanish) there is a well-known saying for which I've not found a good English equivalent: "The devil is more devious by reason of his advanced age than by reason of his devilishness" (my translation of "mas sabe el diablo por viejo que por diablo"). I confess that when I first heard it from my grandmother, I was skeptical, like every other pre-adult who ever walked the earth. Today, my skepticism has dwindled.

6. **They think a subject or circumstance is so unprecedented that no advice seems worthwhile.**

Sometimes circumstances really are unprecedented, especially in connection with new technologies. *Should I try to get into a new technology field? Should I start a business in this field?* Recent examples of life-changing technologies include the Web and mobile communication devices. We can expect more life-changing technologies, such as in biomedicine.

However, most decisions that could benefit from advice do not involve new technologies. Instead, they involve timeless issues of human relationships or life choices that have been faced by others many times before. As Chapter 2 points out, the value of advice is not necessarily in being given a *solution* but in seeing the choices in new ways, or even in learning about a factor that has not occurred to you, such as, "*What will happen when you have children if you buy a house in this neighborhood?*"—a question that may not occur to a childless couple who are first-time home buyers.

7. **The issue doesn't seem important or difficult enough to go to the trouble of seeking advice.**

Many issues aren't worth the trouble. Seeking advice does impose somewhat on one's advisors, especially if there isn't a strong relationship with them, or if the relationship has been mostly one-sided, so that you have not helped your advisor with his or her issues within your capabilities. The way to increase the number of issues you can practically seek advice on is to enlarge your circle of potential advisors, for example, by following old advice of Dale Carnegie in his classic book *How to Win Friends and Influence People*: Do things for people without seeking anything in return.

The rise of the World Wide Web has solved the problem of finding solutions for narrowly scoped problems, and is making inroads on broader issues as well. The threshold for advice seeking has moved upwards, emphasizing issues for which one's personal circumstances matter. A later chapter will examine the question of the appropriate scope of Web and social media as sources of advice versus personal, one-on-one advice.

> 8. **A viable option is to do nothing, even if it's not the best option, so they neither seek advice on positive actions nor take any positive actions even without seeking advice, due to the comfort of inertia.**

Sometimes it's most comfortable to do nothing and see what happens: to let matters run their course. Health problems and interpersonal conflicts are common examples of this, and generally anytime the current state of affairs is unsatisfactory but is not disabling, urgent, or deteriorating fast.

> 9. **A low level of knowledge—whether in general or specific to the problem—causes people to "not know what they don't know" and fail to recognize that they have a knowledge or experience gap.**

Besides the emotional immaturity specific to youth, I believe that this factor helps to explain why young people don't seek advice—it's because they have not developed sustained expertise in a subject and applied that expertise to complicated non-classroom issues. Therefore, they are less aware of the presence of knowledge gaps and the importance and practicality of filling them.

> 10. **The tremendous amount of information and opinion on the Web, as well as the rise of social media, leads people to think that those are good enough sources of guidance.**

The Web and social media have enlarged the scope of problems that can be solved without the need for an attentive dialogue with other people. For such anonymous or quasi-anonymous channels, the most suitable problems are those that don't depend on one's individual circumstances. A good example is figuring out what to do if your printer signals an error, or what replacement part is needed for a 10-year-old dishwasher that is no longer sold. The opposite cases, which are not amenable to canned advice, typically depend on the advice seeker's goals, constraints, resources, timelines, fears, and so on. A later chapter will scope out the differences in more detail.

Emotional Reasons

11. They believe that seeking advice shows weakness.

Men probably don't ask for directions, if this truism is actually true, because of this factor. Asking for helpful advice is contrary to the image of the strong, independent, can-do individual who is traditionally admired in most or all cultures. Many studies have "highlighted the reluctance of males to seek help from medical and counseling professionals" (M. Lehdonvirta et al. in *Games and Culture*, vol. 7, no. 1, January 2012).

But it's easy to argue why advice seeking shouldn't be seen as weakness or indecisiveness, because we are interdependent in so many ways, whether verbally or transactionally. After all, even the most self-reliant individual drives an automobile designed and built by others, consumes food that was skillfully produced by farmers, and goes to a doctor for treatment when he is sick. Society has a large number of typical situations where convention dictates that relying on others is absolutely fine. But there is no reason to limit these situations to the conventional types. On the contrary, the strong individual should not fear to draw on outside wisdom. Advice seeking should be seen and felt as the realm of the strong and self-confident who see themselves not as "Lone Rangers". who go it alone, but as entrepreneurs whose task is to bring the world's collective wisdom to bear on their circumstances.

The *U.S. Army Noncommissioned Officer Guide* published on December 23, 2002, in a section on mentorship, states, "Seeking advice or assistance from a mentor is not a sign of weakness, but is evidence of a desire to become a better soldier and leader." The wording signals that mentorship is an acceptable advisory relationship, whereas our viewpoint here is that all relationships can be sources of advice, not just official mentors.

12. They just want the freedom to make their own mistakes, come what may.

There is something to be said for this as a lifestyle choice (see the writings of Emerson later in this book). But it's harder to justify it when you have responsibilities to dependent family or to co-workers who rely on you for well-chosen, effective decisions rather than on your following your tastes and whims. Even with no responsibilities except to yourself, if the goal is effectiveness in maintaining an autonomous lifestyle, then advice has value.

Moreover, seeking advice doesn't eliminate the opportunities for making mistakes! It's still up to you to decide the final course of action as well as to call on good advisors rather than mistaken ones. There is plenty of scope for autonomy and error: how to approach advisors, whom to approach, what to say to them, following up with them, reconciling contradictory advice, and so on. So there is no shortage of learning opportunities!

13. By temperament, they prefer to take action rather than to reflect and think things through.

I agree that it's important to be true to yourself and your best instincts. However, one must realize that advice seeking in *conventional circumstances* doesn't seem to conflict with anyone's temperament. For example, suppose your complicated car makes a terrible racket: Do you take action (what action?) based on your temperament, or do you seek expert advice from a competent mechanic? Suppose you are diagnosed with a rare, complex malady that has no easy solution. Do you go with your instinct, or do you consult medical specialists? Since nearly everyone would consult a specialist, it's important to realize that even creatures of instinct aren't as instinctive as they believe they are *when it really counts*. So the issue is not one of absolute surrender to temperament but where one draws the line based on the trade-off between effectiveness and trueness to self.

14. The courses of action lead to a clear-cut success or failure, which would become known to others if advice were sought.

I believe this is a frequent reason, although I didn't consider it until I had lunch with a colleague, a prolific author of technical computer books, whose experiences I wanted to learn from in writing this book, although our circumstances were different. He had written his first book in response to an express solicitation from a publisher to write a book that provided an introduction to a specific technical subject.

My colleague shared a story about an acquaintance of his who, for reasons of "pridefulness," had not sought his or anyone else's advice when trying to get a book published. That is, it was possible that the book wouldn't be accepted by any publisher, which would be perceived as a failure by others, so better not to seek advice and to keep the attempt under wraps to avoid possible embarrassment. The acquaintance ended up going with a "vanity" publisher, who will publish your book if you pay them, and he later wondered why the publisher made no attempt to promote the work after its publication.

Folk wisdom tries to forestall this timidity: *Nothing ventured, nothing gained.* Or as my mother often said: *The worst attempt is the one that is never undertaken.*

15. They avoid reaching out because of shyness, not for any practical or intellectual reasons.

During a workshop for students at Carnegie Mellon University's Career and Professional Development Center, a young woman asked me about shyness as a barrier to approaching others for advice. Shyness is harder to overcome than reasons that are based on practical or intellectual considerations, which can be trumped using arguments based on effectiveness. But for shyness, just saying *"Don't be shy—it's not effective!"* won't work.

My friend and colleague Anne McCafferty helped with my reply to the student, recommending that shy people build social capital—cordial human relationships that can lead to mutual aid—by building upon their personal interests in events and activities that they feel passionate about. Working through those interests, they can develop cordial relationships within a comfortable context. Another approach is Dale Carnegie's *How to Win Friends and Influence People*, which recommends showing a genuine interest in people and giving of yourself without any expectation of an immediate benefit.

But building social capital takes time. In the short term, a shy person can approach someone for advice by email or regular paper letter. The worst that can happen is that there is no reply.

16. The situation involves confidential or embarrassing details that people prefer not to share, because word could spread beyond the advisor, and even discussing the issue only with an advisor is discomfiting enough.

It's easy for everyone to imagine personal or family issues, medical and otherwise, that one would not be inclined to discuss with a doctor or lawyer,

40

much less with someone who is not bound by professional practice and ethics to uphold confidentiality and be non-judgmental. An advisor should always be told whether a matter is confidential, although people invariably like to talk. Very personal trade-offs between privacy and getting external help are at issue. We could cite Hamlet's famed soliloquy:

> To be, or not to be, that is the question:
> Whether 'tis nobler in the mind to suffer
> The slings and arrows of outrageous fortune,
> Or to take arms against a sea of troubles,
> And by opposing end them?

Hamlet contemplates suicide, but we only consider asking for advice!

> **17. People like to display consistency, so they persist alone in a failed situation in order to avoid publicly changing course.**

If it's the wrong path, consider stopping to ask for directions! There is another relevant saying: *Don't throw* good *money after bad.*

> **18. Their minds are already made up, so they avoid asking for advice for fear that others would contradict their decision.**

This reason was pointed out by a friend who recalled her decision years earlier to withdraw from dental school after three years of study. She didn't consult anyone as she made her decision because she knew that she would have gotten contrary opinions that she didn't want to deal with. This might not be as crazy as it appears. If you *know* you will carry out an irrevocable action, then not listening to naysayers may at least give you peace of mind. Ignorance is sometimes bliss.

> **19. They fear that involving an advisor may lead to a loss of control that could spiral into an undesirable outcome.**

I learned of this reason from the book *The Wise Advisor* by J. W. Salacuse, a law professor at the Fletcher School of Law and Diplomacy at Tufts University. Salacuse writes for an audience of advisors, not our advice seekers, but of course there is overlap. Salacuse wrote, "Sick people resist becoming patients because they fear that their doctors, not they, will control their lives. Seeking a lawyer's help in a dispute with your neighbor may lead to a lawsuit that you never thought you would ever initiate." Salacuse cautions advisors to recognize this fear and reassure their clients that the clients remain in control of their problem and their lives.

> 20. **Their school training led them to attempt (homework) problems by themselves before seeking help, so they carry over that learned behavior to real-life problems, which unlike homework are not done as practice for a test!**

If schoolwork included more training in what psychologists call the *meta-cognitive* skills of "planning, monitoring, and regulating" their own mental activities, then students would be better able to recognize the difference between structured, homework-style problems and the unstructured problems of real life, and adjust their attitudes accordingly.

Social Reasons

> 21. **They believe that others dislike giving advice and thus are reluctant to ask.**

I think people under-appreciate that others, especially those with whom one has an established cordial relationship, or who personally like the advice seeker, are often pleased to give counsel and are flattered to be sought out expressly for this purpose. For sure, there are exceptions among the very busy.

However, nobody likes to give advice when there is an ulterior motive, so be sincere and don't, for example, contact others to look for a job under the guise of seeking advice. People easily see through this and will think less of you.

Consider this simple, humble approach: "I'm facing an important decision and am seeking help in thinking things through. Could we meet briefly so I can get your thoughts (or pick your brain, etc.)?" Nobody of your acquaintance except an ogre or a highly time-pressed individual would dislike being approached like that. Generally, people *love* to give advice when they are approached earnestly and sincerely.

In an article in the *Journal of Personality and Social Psychology* ("If You Need Help, Just Ask: Underestimating Compliance with Direct Requests for Help"), Columbia University researchers F. J. Flynn and V. K. B. Lake found that "people generally underestimate the likelihood of compliance in making a direct request for help, in part, because they fail to fully appreciate that while it is difficult for help-seekers to risk rejection, it is also difficult for potential helpers to offer rejection ... success in help-seeking may be more likely than we tend to assume."

22. They don't want to impose on others' time or goodwill.

Some people are reluctant to impose on others out of a keen sense of courtesy. I would count my own mother in this category.

I will never forget a favorite saying of my advisor in graduate school, the late Herbert A. Simon, the 1978 Nobel Laureate in Economics: "If you want to get something done, approach someone who's busy." He meant that busy people know how to get multiple things done in parallel. That's why they're busy!

23. They don't know whom to ask.

Not everyone is fortunate enough to have access to knowledgeable and wise family, friends, or congenial acquaintances. Sociologists use the term *social capital* for the network of people that one can tap for help or other social interactions. However, even young people whose social standing or age doesn't enable ready access to likely advisors can extend their social networks through their teachers, for example, who often are happy to guide earnest and eager students.

24. Nobody else seems knowledgeable about their situation.

Even people who have a large amount of social capital—social networks that can be tapped in a variety of circumstances—sometimes face circumstances that seem to be outside the experience of everyone within one's circle. In the story in Chapter 1 of Conrad, the foreign student with an all-expense-paid scholarship to any American university that would accept him, maybe Conrad didn't know any engineers himself, although it's likely that someone he knew also knew an engineer, so his social network that was available for advice extended beyond his immediate circle of family, friends, and acquaintances. In my own case of applying to master's program as a graduating senior, I did not know anyone socially who had done what I was seeking to do, but I could easily have called on teaching assistants, professors, or others who had regular contact with undergraduates and had their own personal experience with admissions.

25. They avoid consulting others in authority over them, such as a workplace superior or their parents, because they don't want to feel obligated to follow their advice or risk causing offense.

This reason was brought to my attention by the CFO of a public company who explained how he tends to avoid asking his boss (the CEO) for advice because his boss might resent it if the advice isn't followed. As we saw in Chapter 2 on what advice really consists of, this situation might be remedied if one asked the boss not for solutions to one's problem, but instead for other helpful input that advice seekers can get from advisors, input that does not lead to clear-cut *did follow* or *did not follow* type outcomes which can cause resentment.

Educational psychologists make this distinction between so-called *executive* and *instrumental* help; executive help provides answers and solutions, whereas instrumental help deals with processes toward finding solutions.

26. They may not want to share credit with others for their subsequent accomplishments.

To counteract this tendency, it helps to realize that everything that one knows builds upon the accomplishments of others. One can borrow from earlier wisdoms: *No man is an island*, wrote the 17th-century English poet John Donne. It is said that President Ronald Reagan's desk in the Oval Office contained a plaque that read: *There is no limit to what a man can do if he does not mind who gets the credit.*

Biological Reasons

27. Cultural factors, particularly for those in the United States who came from other countries, may discourage advice seeking for varying reasons.

A later chapter on cross-cultural aspects of advice seeking will examine these factors in more detail, drawing on insights from scholarly research articles. For example, East Asians may be concerned with negative social outcomes from the advisory process and thus avoid involving their social networks in their problems. On the other hand, Russians may get so much unsolicited advice from friends and family that they feel no need to deliberately seek it.

28. Biological research reveals that adolescents, unlike children and adults, are risk-prone, and that certain genes predispose some people to seek social support and others to avoid it.

Experiments at Cornell and Stanford Universities by B. J. Casey, A. Galvan, and their co-workers suggest that the *drive to act* in teens, not yet developed during early childhood, is in turn not yet balanced by a *restraint system*, which only kicks in during the early twenties. Adolescents may not seek advice—not because they are inexperienced in judging risk/reward or anticipating the future—but because they are emotionally prone to unrestrained risk-taking.

It would not be too surprising if one's genetic makeup had an influence, since it seems to influence just about everything else in one's body and psyche. Interestingly, cultural norms seem to interact with genes in subtle ways, as will be discussed in Chapter 15, "Advice Seeking in Different Cultures." However, even if genetics predisposes us, advice seeking is an act that is subject to rational choice and analysis. To paraphrase an ancient devotional proverb ("man proposes but God disposes"), *biology predisposes but people dispose.*

Summarizing: This chapter has listed 28 reasons for not seeking advice, partly to help recognize ourselves in them and partly to marshal counter-arguments, item by item. The single most common reason is that advice seeking just doesn't occur to people except in conventional cases. Usually none of these reasons is good enough to justify not seeking advice.

We have now finished our survey of the landscape by identifying the potential gains from reaching the destination and working through the reasons that keep people away from the journey. The next chapters will review scouting reports from earlier travelers: other self-improvement authors, researchers, and folk wisdom.

Chapter 4: What Advice Books Say

Advice books, which advise their readers on myriad subjects, including cooking, romance, happiness, business success, weight loss, careers, writing, getting published—are a major industry. For example, the *New York Times* lists bestsellers in various book categories according to subject matter, form of the book (picture books, hardcover, e-book), and others. As of this writing, the *Times* bestseller list includes only one nonfiction *subject* category, "Advice & Misc.," which shows the readership that self-help books attract, at least in U.S. culture.

Just what do these advice books do for you? One blogger on the Web wrote, "The best advice books are the ones that tell you everything you already knew you should be doing but aren't. But when that very same information is presented to you in the book, this time it is presented in a way that clicks." My initial thought was that this sounds right; after further thought, however, I think it's wrong.

Books that reinforce what you already know, but make it all click, are *inspirational* books. Using eloquent language, vivid examples, and moving anecdotes, they inspire you to do what you know how to do but otherwise might not do. Biographies of famous achievers are like that. Through depictions of courage, tenacity, and intrepidness, they inspire readers to emulate these people in their own lives, although everyone already knows that courage and perseverance are virtues! No, the value of the best advice books is that they don't just inspire—they teach. They teach new ways of seeing aspects of the world or of human relations, or new methods or techniques that enable greater health, happiness, or effectiveness.

There is a long history of self-help, self-improvement, and advice books that use ethical principles to teach methods of effective action. An example from pre-Christian Roman antiquity is Marcus Tullius Cicero's *On Friendship*, which I read as a young adult. Likewise, Cicero's book on oratory is a practical guide for persuasion based on principles, not mere technique. The Bible is of course a paragon of ethics-driven self-improvement.

The U.S. origins of self-help literature can be traced to Benjamin Franklin's *Poor Richard's Almanack* and Franklin's autobiography. In her 2004 doctoral thesis, *Self-Help Books and the Quest for Self-Control in the United States 1950-2000*, Christine Whelan at the University of Oxford writes:

> In the late eighteenth and early nineteenth centuries, Benjamin Franklin (1706-1790) and other more secular writers entered the advice business, offering tips for success through virtue. In his *Autobiography* (1791/3), Franklin includes a self-help section that envisions success as something achieved through intrinsic qualities of industriousness, not extrinsic achievements in politics or war. At its most basic, for these early writers, success was only achievable through the development of good character. In many ways, Franklin was the patron saint of the self-help movement.

The term "self-help" is credited to the Scotsman Samuel Smiles, whose life was described by T. H. E. Travers in a 1977 *Albion* article, "Samuel Smiles and the Origins of "Self-Help": Reform and the New Enlightenment." Travers writes:

> Samuel Smiles' popular book *Self-Help* (1859) is usually cited as a convenient example of mid-Victorian individualism and middle class values.
> [...]
> Samuel Smiles' "gospel" of self-help has been variously interpreted, most frequently in terms of a gospel of success, although the single-minded pursuit of wealth and social status always earned Smiles' severest censure ..."

According to Travers, Smiles assumed that:

> ... although environmental influences were extremely powerful, especially in youth, they were not overwhelming and could be reversed to a considerable extent by the personal efforts of the adult. [...] Smiles accepted the concept that the final goal in life for the individual, upon which individual happiness depended, lay in the exercise and fullest possible development of the faculties—physical, moral, and intellectual—so that man, as a rational being, could fulfill the high purposes for which he was Divinely created. As Smiles put it, to "raise man, on earth, to the very summit of his nature."

Finally, the *Forbes* magazine publisher and columnist Rich Karlgaard described the 20th-century development of American self-help culture in an article, "Self-Help: The Great American Religion," in the April 11, 2011 issue of the magazine:

> Out of the depths of the Great Depression came a modern American religion that still exerts a powerful influence. It has two strands.

Karlgaard's one strand, focused on character, led to the 1935 founding of Alcoholics Anonymous. The other strand, more focused on financial success, led to Napoleon Hill's 1937 book *Think and Grow Rich*.

This chapter will examine the self-help writings of three authors whose work spanned more than a century and who have had a major impact on self-improvement/self-help literature and the culture as a whole.

The 7 Habits of Highly Effective People

A hugely successful advice book is *The 7 Habits of Highly Effective People*, which has sold more than 15 million copies worldwide and was written by the late business consultant and professor Stephen R. Covey. *7 Habits* tries to provide a total system of interpersonal living, focusing on character development as the seed from which the roots of effective human relationships, the branches of attitudes, skills, and habits, and the flowers of success and happiness spring.

Covey's ambitious book addresses human relations as a whole, but it doesn't directly try to encourage advice seeking nor to teach how to do it. Covey's *7 Habits* does help his readers become better advice *givers*, which is very relevant to us, since a key aspect of advice seeking is being able to recognize good advice givers, perhaps those who have read Covey's book!

Covey's Habit 5, Seek First to Understand, Then to Be Understood, is introduced with a parable about a patient going to see an optometrist:

> Suppose you've been having trouble with your eyes and you decide to go to an optometrist for help. After briefly listening to your complaint, he takes off his glasses and hands them to you.
>
> "Put these on," he says. "I've worn this pair of glasses for ten years now and they've really helped me. I have an extra pair at home; you can wear these."
>
> So you put them on, but it only makes the problem worse.
>
> "This is terrible!" you exclaim. I can't see a thing!"
>
> "Well, what's wrong?" he asks. "They work great for me. Try harder."
>
> "I am trying," you insist. "Everything is a blur."
>
> "Well, what's the matter with you? Think positively."
>
> "Okay. I positively can't see a thing."
>
> "Boy, are you ungrateful!" he chides. "And after all I've done to help you!"

> What are your chances that you'd go back to that optometrist the next time you needed help? Not very good, I would imagine. You don't have much confidence in someone who doesn't diagnose before he or she prescribes.

Covey summarizes the single most important principle that he has learned in the field of interpersonal communications: "Seek first to understand, then to be understood." He adds: "Although it's risky and hard, seek first to understand, or diagnose before you prescribe, is a correct principle manifest in many areas of life. It's the mark of all true professionals."

Covey gives two scenarios of a father/son dialogue, sparked by the son's complaint about school being "for the birds." The first scenario is marked by the well-meaning father's scolding remarks, which are a projection of his own autobiography—Covey's term for life experience—onto his son, and by the father's general failure to understand the details of his son's circumstances, as well as his son's feelings about them, before giving his reactions to his son.

In the second scenario—one that is *empathic*—Covey's father figure shows that he understands what his son is saying, rephrases the son's remarks, develops the logic of the situation but diverges into the emotional plane when the son does, and withholds judgment or recommendation until he truly understands his son.

It's easy to imagine that this first scenario is very common, although not quite to the hapless extreme shown by the father, because empathic listening is hard and unfamiliar. It's much easier to launch into telling one's own story based on a quick cue or two. After all, there is widespread training in debate and in public speaking, but not as much training in private listening and diagnosis. We've all heard of debate societies and public-speaking clubs, but has anyone ever heard of a listening club?

Covey states that as the father begins to give counsel in the empathic scenario, he needs to be sensitive to his son's communication. As long as his son's response is logical, the father can effectively ask questions and give counsel. But the moment the son's response becomes emotional, the father needs to go back to empathic listening. Also, empathic encounters aren't isolated events, but are part of an ongoing relationship in which deposits are made into an Emotional Bank Account, allowing for trust and withdrawals in future situations.

According to Covey, a highly effective person is an empathic listener, because that person is able to develop excellent trust-based relationships in which a parent can counsel a child or a businessperson can seal a deal with a prospective customer. Covey's business examples show that the thrust of empathic listening is not just to be an effective advisor to one's family but to be more effective at many types of human relationships, including work-based ones.

Other passages from *7 Habits* are extremely relevant to our purpose:

> To relate effectively with a wife, a husband, children, friends, or working associates, we must learn to listen. And this requires emotional strength. Listening involves patience, openness, and the desire to understand—highly developed qualities of character. It's so much easier to operate from a low emotional level and to give high-level advice.
>
> Unless you're influenced by my uniqueness, I'm not going to be influenced by your advice. So if you want to be really effective in the habit of interpersonal communication, you cannot do it with technique alone. You have to build the skills of empathic listening on a base of character that inspires openness and trust.
>
> All the well-meaning advice in the world won't amount to a hill of beans if we're not even addressing the real problem. And we'll never get to the problem if we're so caught up in our own autobiography, our own paradigms, that we don't take off our glasses long enough to see the world from another point of view.
>
> But unless I open up with you, unless you understand me and my unique situation and feelings, you won't know how to advise or counsel me. What you say is good and fine, but it doesn't quite pertain to me.

Covey convincingly shows that advice giving is hard, experts are few, and that advice giving is a learnable skill. The key to giving advice effectively is to understand the advice seeker's unique person and circumstances. Throughout this book, we will build on this insight to develop ways to recognize good advice givers and to help them become even better at giving advice.

The advisory process in Covey's *7 Habits* can be summarized in this way: To advise well, first listen well.

Self-Reliance According to Emerson and Thoreau

A strain in American literary culture dating from the mid-19th century is the self-reliance of Henry David Thoreau, who went to live by himself at Walden Pond in Massachusetts, and of Ralph Waldo Emerson, who also was a proponent of self-reliance and wrote an essay by that name. Thoreau and Emerson are studied in U.S. high schools and have influenced generations of Americans. I was assigned to read their works in my own high school in Chicago's suburbs and still remember the lively discussion that their themes roused in my fellow students and me.

Ralph Waldo Emerson

To understand what this strain of self-reliance implies about advice seeking as we conceive of it here, I undertook to read Emerson's essay *Self-Reliance*, first published in 1841. What I found was a tirade against the idea of interconnectedness and collaboration—against the idea of building upon what has been achieved before—quite the opposite of Isaac Newton's (the famed

17th–18th century discoverer of the laws of motion in physics) "standing on the shoulders of giants."

Emerson formulates a principle that individuals should rely on themselves rather than on "sages" or experts:

> A man should learn to detect and watch that gleam of light which flashes across his mind from within, more than the lustre of the firmament of bards and sages.

Within the same essay he reinforces the idea less metaphorically:

> Every decent and well-spoken individual affects and sways me more than is right. It is easy in the world to live after the world's opinion; it is easy in solitude to live after our own; but the great man is he who in the midst of the crowd keeps with perfect sweetness the independence of solitude.

For Emerson, autonomy and even solitude trump effectiveness, as shown in these excerpts from the same essay:

> I know that for myself it makes no difference whether I do or forbear those actions which are reckoned excellent.
>
> [...]
>
> A foolish consistency is the hobgoblin of little minds, adored by little statesmen and philosophers and divines. With consistency a great soul has simply nothing to do. He may as well concern himself with his shadow on the wall. Speak what you think now in hard words, and to-morrow speak what to-morrow thinks in hard words again, though it contradict every thing you said to-day. — "Ah, so you shall be sure to be misunderstood." — Is it so bad, then, to be misunderstood? Pythagoras was misunderstood, and Socrates, and Jesus, and Luther, and Copernicus, and Galileo,

and Newton, and every pure and wise spirit that ever took flesh. To be great is to be misunderstood.

Man is timid and apologetic; he is no longer upright; he dares not say "I think," "I am," but quotes some saint or sage. He is ashamed before the blade of grass or the blowing rose. These roses under my window make no reference to former roses or to better ones; they are for what they are [...] There is simply the rose; it is perfect in every moment of its existence.

Emerson summarizes his practical advice here:

Insist on yourself; never imitate. Your own gift you can present every moment with the cumulative force of a whole life's cultivation; but of the adopted talent of another, you have only an extemporaneous, half possession. That which each can do best, none but his Maker can teach him. No man yet knows what it is, nor can, till that person has exhibited it. Where is the master who could have taught Shakespeare? Where is the master who could have instructed Franklin, or Washington, or Bacon, or Newton? Every great man is a unique. The Scipionism of Scipio is precisely that part he could not borrow. Shakespeare will never be made by the study of Shakespeare.

At no point in his essay does Emerson come out and say, "Never seek advice," much less say that "pathetic advice seeking is the hobgoblin of little minds." Nor does he say directly that it is better to rely on oneself and fail than to rely on others and succeed. However, such an attitude—basically, a lifestyle choice—is wholly consistent with the plain text and overall tone of Emerson's essay.

As for Henry David Thoreau, his book *Walden* doesn't mince words, although he does make mincemeat of his seniors:

> Age is no better, hardly so well, qualified for an instructor as youth, for it has not profited so much as it has lost. One may almost doubt if the wisest man has learned anything of absolute value by living. Practically, the old have no very important advice to give the young, their own experience has been so partial, and their lives have been such miserable failures, for private reasons, as they must believe; and it may be that they have some faith left which belies that experience, and they are only less young than they were. I have lived some thirty years on this planet, and I have yet to hear the first syllable of valuable or even earnest advice from my seniors. They have told me nothing, and probably cannot tell me anything to the purpose. Here is life, an experiment to a great extent untried by me; but it does not avail me that they have tried it. If I have any experience which I think valuable, I am sure to reflect that this my Mentors said nothing about.

One wonders if Emerson ever achieved something that required complicated teamwork, or faced a course of action whose potentially negative outcome outweighed the positive feelings from acting self-reliantly. Emerson made a living first as a teacher, then as a minister, and finally after the age of 30 as a lecturer and essayist. He also inherited a fair sum after the death at age 20 of his first wife from the then-scourge of tuberculosis. Emerson made a living through the articulateness and provocativeness of his nonconformist opinions, an occupation that was enhanced by his championing of self-reliance. One doubts whether other occupations, or even practical affairs like seeking the best treatments for tuberculosis, were enhanced by the same beliefs.

Emerson's essay *Self-Reliance*, which he might have entitled *Advice is for Losers,* is not forgotten. Amazon.com's The Domino Project, started in late 2010 as a foray into book publishing, included Emerson's essay among the small number of initial book titles. As I write this in 2012, President Barack Obama's Facebook page lists *Self-Reliance* as a Favorite Book among eight entries.

How to Win Friends and Influence People

Dale Carnegie's *How to Win Friends and Influence People*, first published in 1936, is a standard-bearer among self-help books. Its language and examples were updated in a 1981 revision in which two sections were dropped. (I'll soon be quoting from one of those sections, though.) I first read this book while in my early twenties and was impressed with its principles for governing human relations. None of the principles is novel, and all of them depend heavily on looking at interactions from the other's viewpoint and judging what interaction style is most effective.

The book is marred for me slightly by a somewhat cynical view of human self-centeredness and by the large number of sales-oriented anecdotes, for example, those about dealing well with people in order to make a sale. However, the book evolved from Carnegie's in-person courses taken often by business people, so the sales-related examples are understandable. Overall, Carnegie's highly readable book is a gem of principles of positive human relations, supported by liberal quotations of eminent authors and public figures and made vivid by many anecdotes from his students and historical examples. Our question here is: What does Carnegie's book teach about advice seeking?

Carnegie seeks to improve his readers' effectiveness in dealing with others, but he also wants to improve his readers' own emotional satisfaction in those dealings. Carnegie doesn't directly address advice seeking, but he touches on it in some cases. For example, Carnegie's Part 5 on writing effective letters ("Letters That Produced Miraculous Results"—from the original edition) teaches readers to ask others—with genuine sincerity—for small favors that draw on their knowledge. Carnegie's examples include both sides of the "prestige" relation: when the advice seeker is socially "superior" to the giver as well as when the giver is more important than oneself. Carnegie tells the story of a trip to rural France before World War II:

> Homer Croy and I once lost our way while motoring through the interior of France. Halting our old Model T, we asked a group of peasants how we could get to the next big town.
>
> The effect of the question was electrical. These peasants, wearing wooden shoes, regarded all Americans as rich. And

> automobiles were rare in those regions, extremely rare. Americans touring through France in a car! Surely we must be millionaires. Maybe cousins of Henry Ford. But they knew something we didn't know. We had more money than they had; but we had to come to them hat in hand to find out how to get to the next town. And that gave them a feeling of importance. They all started talking at once. One chap, thrilled at this rare opportunity, commanded the others to keep quiet. He wanted to enjoy all alone the thrill of directing us.
>
> Try this yourself. The next time you are in a strange city, stop someone who is below you in the economic and social scale and say: "I wonder if you would mind helping me out of a little difficulty. Won't you please tell me how to get to such and such a place?"

For Carnegie, advice seeking is a means to the end of building a good human relationship, whereas we treat advice seeking as a means to solve a specific problem. Building a good human relationship is a side benefit, but it isn't this book's focus. From our narrower standpoint, we could call Carnegie's book *Getting Advice Helps You Win Friends and Influence People*.

Another Carnegie example is from sales, where the advice seeker, the salesperson, is in the subordinate position. Carnegie tells the story of Mr. Amsel, who sold plumbing and heating materials, and his efforts to win the business of a Brooklyn plumber. Amsel had no luck until the time he consulted the plumber about the wisdom of Amsel's employer opening a new branch store in a neighborhood that the plumber knew well. After that session, the plumber became a customer and the two of them established a business friendship.

For our purposes, Carnegie's point is that people are often happy to share their knowledge when approached in the right way, regardless of who, if anyone, holds the dominant position.

Carnegie takes pains to point out that the principles and methods that his book puts forward aren't just stratagems or tricks but a different way of thinking about human relations. He writes:

> Let me repeat: the principles taught in this book will work only when they come from the heart. I am not advocating a bag of tricks. I am talking about a new way of life.

This is true of all the *good* self-help books: They intend to teach how to be a better, more satisfied person at the same time as they teach how to be an effective person, in both our personal and working lives. *Advice is for Winners* has the same aspiration.

We've now looked at a sample of the self-help writings of several prominent American authors that span more than a century. Only Emerson's and Thoreau's essays directly address advice seeking, whereas the advisory process is peripheral to Covey's and Carnegie's larger goals of effective and productive human relationships. Summarizing what we learned about advice:

- To advise well, first listen well. (Covey)
- Advice is for losers. (Emerson)
- Nobody has anything of value to tell me. (Thoreau)
- Getting advice helps you win friends and influence people. (Carnegie)

None of these teaches the reader to be more proactive and skilled at advice seeking, our goal here. Covey gives a clue for recognizing good advisors, Emerson and Thoreau say to forget the whole thing, and Carnegie teaches how to build lasting relationships, which are a valuable resource for those seeking advice.

Our first of three scouting reports was from trailblazing predecessors whose insights are relevant to advice seeking, although not always directly concerned with that topic. As we have seen, Emerson's and Thoreau's recommendations are not at all to our taste. The next chapter's scouting report is from the scholarly research literature.

Chapter 5: What Research Says

Academic researchers study just about everything under the sun. Take baseball, for example. How much baseball-related research can you guess is done by, say, scholarly researchers in the field of biomedicine? It turns out that well over 600 scholarly articles in biomedicine have been written that mention baseball in the article titles! Here are just three:

- Researchers at Louisiana Tech, Cal State Fullerton, Texas Christian, and Cal State Sacramento have studied the effects of warm-up technique, grip, and physiology on hitters' bat velocity when swinging at the ball.

- Taiwanese researchers have studied the effects of medial elbow pain on throwing kinematics among adolescent baseball players.

- Researchers at the University of Miami conducted an in-depth study of pick-off moves by left-handed pitchers.

I expected that researchers have had something to say about the advisory process, and I was not disappointed. Most often, advice taking and advice seeking has been studied by psychologists, sociologists, business authors, and health and educational professionals who look at knowledge transfer between medical and teaching peers and patients. This chapter will present and interpret some of what has been learned by scholars about advice.

Advice seeking is less studied than advice taking because *taking* is more prone to measurement. For example, by how much did the advice *taker* in a laboratory experiment change some numerical decision, like offering a bid at auction, in response to a specific recommendation? Advice seeking, on the other hand, is a subject of best practices, with less scope for measurement and statistics.

My own graduate school advisor taught me that when trying to make sense of poorly understood areas of human activity, it helps to identify what are the basic phenomena—or "hard facts" that serve as an anchor in order to avoid excessive drift. Scientists keep their eye on hard facts as the object of their explanatory theories. For example, if someone proposes a new theory, other scientists check if it can account for the hard facts. Of course, people can disagree on whether purported hard facts are indeed hard or actually soft. In my own research on how the creative discoveries made by scientists could be enhanced with computers, one of the few hard facts about discovery is that, according to self-reports, breakthrough ideas happen while the discoverer was doing something else—washing hands, riding a bicycle, picking out the groceries, and so on. Any theory about how creative discoveries are made should account for the *Aha!* moments of so many breakthrough discoveries. So what hard facts about the advice process have researchers uncovered?

Egocentric Discounting. A widely reported phenomenon of advice taking is called *egocentric discounting*. People tend to partially disregard good advice, which is known to be good because of the design of the laboratory experiment. They may adjust their solutions in the direction of the advisor's recommendation, but only somewhat, as if to seek a compromise between their own "egocentric" preferences and the recommendation. Various explanations of egocentric discounting have been put forth:

- People just prefer their own opinions.

- People aren't given, or don't understand, the reasons that underlie an advisor's recommendation, whereas they do understand their own reasons.

- Initial opinions form mental "anchors" that weigh down the adjustment process as advice or new information is considered.

Forbidden Fruit. Working within a different research specialty, in a 2004 article ("Reactance to Recommendations: When Unsolicited Advice Yields Contrary Responses" in *Marketing Science*) the business school professors G. J. Fitzsimmons and D. R. Lehmann discussed related ideas that I am calling *forbidden fruit*. Here they describe the results of their experiments in consumer choice:

> ... when experts recommend a dominated [*i.e., clearly unattractive*] option or recommend against a dominant [*clearly attractive*] option, decision makers demonstrate reduced satisfaction levels. In this situation, the difference between the decision maker's evaluation of the option and that of the expert sets up a high-conflict decision environment. Most interestingly, we find that when experts recommend against a dominant option, a "reactance-style" response occurs. Decision makers become quite dissatisfied and, rather than adjusting their decisions according to the expert recommendations or simply ignoring them, a backlash occurs such that we observe an increase in the choice of the option that was recommended against.

The authors report their use of the psychological concept of "reactance," writing:

> In his theory of reactance, Brehm (1966) posited that when an individual's freedom is restricted through the elimination of ... a behavior, that individual will experience a state of psychological reactance [which is] a motivational state directed towards reattaining the restricted freedom. The result is ... an increase in the attractiveness of the constrained behavior and a decrease in the evaluation of the source of the restriction, as well as an increased sense of confidence in the ultimate decision made.

In other words, fruit that is forbidden has increased appeal, while its forbidders are resented. Readers of the biblical Book of Genesis as well as parents of teenagers may recognize this phenomenon.

However, Fitzsimmons and Lehmann caution that their experimental subjects formed preferences *before* receiving recommendations, and write, "It is not clear that our results will generalize to situations in which the decision maker receives a recommendation either before or at the same time he or she forms attitudes toward choice options."

Besides research on people's overall discounting of advice, scholars have uncovered individual factors that lead people to accept or disregard advice.

These factors relate to characteristics of the advisor or advice seeker, the advice itself, and the issue that gives rise to the need for advice. Drawing on the 2006 article by S. Bonaccio and R. S. Dalal, "Advice Taking and Decision Making: An Integrative Literature Review, and Implications for the Organizational Sciences" (in *Organizational Behavior and Human Decision Processes*), let's group some of these factors and then discuss a few in more detail later.

The Advisor. Advice seekers tend to heed advice given by advisors who:

1. Have recognizable, relevant expertise.

2. Have a good reputation or have made a good impression on the advice seeker.

3. Are older than the advice seeker.

4. Are well-educated.

5. Have more life experience than the advice seeker or are perceived as wise.

6. Express confidence in their ability to provide sound advice.

7. Follow their own advice. (!)

8. Are likable or liked by the advice seeker.

9. Are physically attractive.

10. Are wealthy or powerful.

11. Are trusted by the advice seeker.

12. Share the seeker's goals.

Advice seekers also tend to disregard advice from those who possess the opposite traits: young, inexperienced, poor, plain, tentative, uneducated, untrustworthy, or having different goals. In addition, some studies have shown that people discount all advice when multiple advisors contradict each other (I. Yaniv and M. Milyavsky in "Using Advice from Multiple Sources to Revise and Improve Judgments" *in Organizational Behavior and Human Decision*

Processes, 2007) and that people's confidence in their final judgments is low when their advisors disagree.

Some of these advisor characteristics are related: People tend to like others who are physically attractive, and wealthy people tend to have power in the sense of arranging their circumstances as they choose. Also, many of these characteristics have little to do with the *quality* of advice. People may reasonably use them as cues to judge quality, but they are not reliable indicators. For example, wealth may suggest accomplishment, which suggests general effectiveness. But what predisposes a wealthy person to give good counsel on selecting a career, repairing a problematic relationship at work, or on the best way to deal with a chronically unruly child?

My own view is that advice giving is a skill like any other. Some people are good at it and others are not, quite apart from their expertise about the issue at hand. Later chapters will refer to the book *The Wise Advisor*, which tries to teach advice-giving skills to consultants and other professionals.

The Advice. Advice seekers tend to heed advice when it:

1. Is (perceptibly) of good quality.

2. Agrees with the advice from others.

3. Comes with a reasoned justification.

4. Is solicited, not unsolicited.

5. Is paid for, rather than obtained free of charge.

Advice seekers tend to discount advice when it comes from peers and is based on intuition, unlike the case of intuitive advice from more senior people, which is more highly regarded. There are also reports of discounting advice that is very different from that of other advisors. Finally, some advice is not only disregarded but actively contradicted when it conflicts with already-formed preferences.

The Advice Seekers. Advice seekers tend to heed advice when they:

1. Are inexperienced, or less experienced than the advisor.

2. Have positive emotions such as gratitude about the advisor due to prior related issues.

3. Feel some shame, for example, about their performance on prior related issues.

Advice seekers also tend to discount advice when they feel pride in their own accomplishments on earlier problems that are similar to the current issue.

The Issue at Hand. Advice seekers tend to heed advice on issues that:

1. Are complex, but to disregard advice on simple issues.

2. Are ill-structured if the offered advice is based on intuition. For example, deciding which of two films a movie studio should agree to finance and produce is an ill-structured problem; a recommendation in favor of one film might be based on a gut feeling. As S. C. Tzioti states in her 2010 doctoral dissertation (*Let Me Give You A Piece of Advice: Empirical Papers about Advice Taking in Marketing*—Erasmus University Rotterdam): "In certain cases [of ill-structured issues and a more senior advisor], justifying advice on the basis of intuition is actually more effective than justifying advice based on analysis."

Unsolicited Advice. On the subject of receptivity to unsolicited advice, Bonaccio and Dalal offer a summary:

> The research, though sparse, indicates rather unambiguously that unsolicited advice is poorly received. It is discounted to a greater extent than explicitly solicited advice ... Moreover, whereas explicitly solicited advice is perceived as cooperative and helpful, unsolicited advice is considered to be intrusive (i.e., an attempt to "butt in"), a form of criticism ... and inappropriate ... Unsolicited help (e.g., advice and/or physical/material help), especially if offered in a directive (i.e., controlling or imposing) manner, may convey to judges [decision-makers] that they are unable to cope with the problem autonomously and may consequently threaten their self-esteem ...

Broader implications. Considerations besides decision quality for the matter at hand are not the only ones relevant to advice taking, as Bonaccio and Dalal point out:

> The aforementioned reasons pertain to decision quality. However, there are also social reasons for taking advice. Sniezek and Buckley (1995) indicated the possibility of social pressure not to reject freely offered advice: Such advice, if rejected, may not be proffered again in the future.

Other chapters of this book have much more to say about the social aspects of advice seeking. One of the reasons cited in Chapter 3, "28 Reasons for Not Seeking Advice," deals with avoiding advice from others who are in a position of authority, not because advice may not be offered again, but because of possible offense if advice isn't followed.

Some research has looked at more general outcomes of advice seeking behaviors. In a 2010 article ("Top Management Team Advice Seeking and Exploratory Innovation: The Moderating Role of TMT Heterogeneity" in the *Journal of Management Studies*), A. S. Alexiev, J. J. P. Jansen, F. A. Van Den Bosch, and H. W. Volberda, collected questionnaire data from small and medium-sized firms in The Netherlands and tested for relationships between a firm's success in exploratory innovation and advice seeking behavior among its top managers. They found a strong correlation, suggesting that advice seeking leads the firms to perform better in uncharted areas like innovation, although the direction of the relationship was not unambiguously determined: Does advice seeking lead to innovation, or does innovation bring advice seeking in its wake?

The book *Executive Intelligence* by Justin Menkes, drawing on the business literature and the author's own consulting practice, identifies three components of superior executive intelligence: "... the accomplishment of tasks, working with and through other people, and judging oneself and adjusting one's behavior accordingly." The last component actually refers to one's knowledge and perspectives, recognizing gaps within them, and plugging those gaps with external help. Menkes elaborates:

Effective executive action always calls for an individual to be able to turn a critical eye on his or her own thinking and behavior. Whether in a strategy-planning meeting, a one-on-one exchange, or any other business format, a leader must be able to test the limits of his or her own ideas against those of others. This is not to suggest that skilled executives are robots who do not feel emotions such as defensiveness, but rather that they can recognize their own mistakes without being blinded by their reactions to them.

Finally, in a 2010 article ("How Resources (or Lack Thereof) Influence Advice Seeking on Psychological Well-Being and Marital Risk: Testing Pathways of the Lack of Financial Stability, Support, and Strain" in the *Journal of Adult Development*), M. Curran, C. Totenhagen, and J. Serido conceive of advice seeking as a *resource depletion*:

One way to conceptualize advice seeking using the model of conservation of resources is that of resource loss: that is, when individuals seek advice from others, they are depleting their resources, such that advice seeking is an act that requires people to use social capital, thus not only incurring a depletion of resources, but also not allowing them to build up their resources. Thus, greater advice seeking should predict a decrease in psychological well-being.

The authors point out that advice seeking could be a *net resource gain* when it involves "an investment of one resource ... to increase another, more valuable resource (e.g., figuring out ways to reduce marital risk)." That is, the obtained advice might lead to improving your well-being more than the cost in social capital (the end result of the establishment of human bonds of goodwill and trust that can be deepened and called upon over time) that it incurs.

I have difficulty with this view. Even if it is true that people generally think that advice seeking imposes a burden on others and so *diminishes* one's future access to support, people should persuade themselves *not* to think that way. On the contrary, advice seeking, when done well, *builds* social capital by enabling mutual satisfaction and deepening social bonds, as mentioned often in this book.

I've reviewed the scholarly research literature on advice seeking and advice taking with several goals in mind:

- To combine my informal observations, personal habits, and business experiences with the insights from academic specialists.

- To understand how advice can guide or derail decision making and how practices vary across cultures.

- To help readers recognize within themselves some of the unfounded biases that these studies reveal and to help them overcome these biases through self-awareness.

- To extract practical recommendations from the phenomena reported by academic studies.

Let's close by reviewing some of the unfounded biases, emotional reactions, and novice mistakes that readers are encouraged to avoid.

- Recognizing "egocentric discounting" as a common occurrence, try to avoid forming opinions before getting advice, or at least try hard to keep an open mind.

- Don't let excess pride in your prior accomplishments prevent you from considering advice in a similar area as those accomplishments.

- Don't let advice that contradicts your formed preferences, or that contradicts other advice, unnerve you (note Chapter 11, "Dealing with Contradictory Advice"). Don't reject contradictory advice out of hand. Don't resent those advisors.

- Try not to be swayed by irrelevant physical attractiveness, wealth, likability, gratitude, and experience, or by facile expressions of advisor overconfidence.

- Unsolicited advice may be unwelcome for emotional reasons. Try to suppress those emotions and instead consider the advisor's motivations as well as the quality of the advice on its merits.

This chapter has provided our second scouting report on the advice-seeking landscape, this time from scholarly researchers. Uniquely, the credibility of research scholarship is based not just on professional experience and wisdom but on experiments, data, and the rigor of needing the approval of one's research peers in order to get published. The final scouting report, in the next chapter, draws its insights from a very different source: the accumulated folk wisdom over centuries of human experience.

Chapter 6: What Proverbs Say

My graduate school advisor (as previously mentioned, the late Herbert A. Simon) was fond of saying that sayings come in contradictory pairs. For example: "Haste makes waste" and "slow and steady wins the race" as opposed to "the early bird gets the worm" and "don't put off for tomorrow what you can do today." I don't believe he meant that sayings are useless but that the circumstances under which they apply need to be examined carefully, case by case. Or perhaps he meant that sayings and proverbs are most useful rhetorically—to argue for a course of action—rather than as a source of reliable wisdom.

Nevertheless, as we investigate how cultures view advice seeking, we should consult mankind's storehouse of proverbs that deal with advice seeking and giving. As raw material, I have consulted various world-wide Web sources, such as QuotationsBook.com, which categorizes proverbs and famous passages into subject areas, one of which is "Advice." Proverbs and quotations are grouped in the following sections according to the messages that they deliver, and I've commented on each one in turn, though there are several different variations of interpretations possible.

Do People Like to Give Advice?

We all admire the wisdom of people who come to us for advice. (Jack Herbert)

> The one thing people are the most liberal with, is their advice. (François de la Rochefoucauld)
>
> In matters of religion and matrimony I never give any advice; because I will not have anybody's torments in this world or the next laid to my charge. (Lord Chesterfield)
>
> Never give anyone the advice to buy or sell shares, because ... the most benevolent piece of advice can turn out badly. (Josef de la Vega)
>
> To offer a man unsolicited advice is to presume that he doesn't know what to do or that he can't do it on his own. (John Gray)

Yes, being asked for advice is flattering, but some topics are uncomfortable and can boomerang on the advice giver. Also, offering unsolicited advice is to be avoided.

In my early twenties, a close friend was a fellow engineering student. He had married young and had two young children, and he had to work to support the family in addition to completing his studies. Given the various stresses, he reached a point of a marital separation, and I listened to my friend as he unburdened himself about his difficulties. Of course, I had no personal experience with his type of situation, but that often doesn't stop us from offering our thoughts. However, I limited myself to offering my ears together with moral support, because even then I envisioned this scenario: After a few months of separation, my friend and his wife would reconcile. If I did anything besides listen, that is, if I offered suggestions or voiced agreement with him about his attitude toward his wife, he might later on resent my having done so, particularly if they reconciled. In fact, they *did* reconcile and stayed together ever after. I was thus very glad that I withheld my own opinions and just listened to him.

As the proverbs warn, tread very carefully on highly emotional marital and religious issues!

What is Good Advice?

> Counsel woven into the fabric of real life is wisdom. (Walter Benjamin)

Good advice is specific and concrete.

> Advice is like snow; the softer it falls the longer it dwells upon, and the deeper it sinks into the mind. (Samuel Taylor Coleridge)
>
> To advise is not to compel. (German proverb)

Good advice is delivered delicately, without taking offense if it is disregarded.

> Whatever advice you give, be short. (Horace)

Good advice is brief.

> Never give advice in a crowd. (Arabian proverb)

Good advice is delivered discreetly without risking public embarrassment.

> Don't follow any advice, no matter how good, until you feel as deeply in your spirit as you think in your mind that the counsel is wise. (David Seabury)

Received advice has to feel right.

> It is bad advice that cannot be changed. (Publilius Syrus)

Advice is always uncertain and tentative.

> If one man says to thee, Thou art a donkey, pay no heed. If two speak thus, purchase a saddle. (The Talmud)

If multiple advisors agree, it's a telling sign.

> Successful men follow the same advice they prescribe for others. (Unknown source)
>
> A pint of example is worth a gallon of advice. (Unknown source)
>
> He that gives good advice, builds with one hand; he that gives good counsel and example, builds with both; but he that gives good admonition and bad example, builds with one hand and pulls down with the other. (Francis Bacon)

Advice is more credible if the advisor also follows it.

Who Are Good Advisors?

> He that has no children brings them up well. (Spanish proverb)

Don't trust the advice of someone with no experience in the subject.

> Never trust the advice of a man in difficulties. (Aesop's fable of the Fox and the Goat)

Self-explanatory.

> The worst men often give the best advice. (Philip James Bailey)

Good advice can come from unexpected sources.

> The best advisers, helpers and friends, always are not those who tell us how to act in special cases, but who give us, out of themselves, the ardent spirit and desire to act right, and leave us then, even through many blunders, to find out what our own form of right action is. (Phillips Brooks)

Good advisors inspire us to find solutions on our own through general principles.

> The advice of the elders to young men is very apt to be as unreal as a list of the hundred best books. (Oliver Wendell Holmes)

Elders may give unrealistic advice to youth (maybe because they've forgotten what being young is like, or because the world has changed sufficiently to invalidate their advice).

> We hate those who will not take our advice, and despise them who do. (Henry Wheeler Shaw)
>
> The true secret of giving advice is, after you have honestly given it, to be perfectly indifferent whether it is taken or not, and never persist in trying to set people right. (Hannah Whitall Smith)

After offering advice, the good advisor accepts whatever course is taken.

> Write down the advice of him who loves you, though you like it not at present. (English proverb)
>
> In friendship, let the influence of friends who give good advice be paramount; and let this influence be used to enforce advice not only in plain-spoken terms, but sometimes, if the case demands it, with sharpness; and when so used, let it be obeyed. (Cicero)

People who care about you give the best advice.

> Never give advice unless asked. (German proverb)

Do not give unsolicited advice.

It's no surprise that some of the sayings contradict each other. On the one hand, experience is helpful. On the other hand, elders sometimes give bad advice to youth. In any case, let's combine of all these into a consensus profile of the good advisor: an experienced, untroubled, humble, caring individual who can convey principles, not just specifics, and who advises only when called upon.

Do People Heed Advice?

We give advice by the bucket, but take it by the grain. (William R. Alger)

In those days he was wiser than he is now—he used frequently to take my advice. (Winston Churchill)

There is hardly a man on earth who will take advice unless he is certain that it is positively bad. (Edward Dahlberg)

Advice is least heeded when most needed. (English proverb)

Wise men don't need advice. Fools won't take it. (Benjamin Franklin)

It takes a great man to give sound advice tactfully, but a greater to accept it graciously. (J. C. Macaulay)

It is an infallible rule that a prince who is not wise himself cannot be well advised. (N. Machiavelli)

I sometimes give myself admirable advice, but I am incapable of taking it. (Lady Mary Wortley Montagu)

Most people who ask for advice from others have already resolved to act as it pleases them. (Khalil Gibran)

They that will not be counseled, cannot be helped. If you do not hear reason she will rap you on the knuckles. (Benjamin Franklin)

The advice that is wanted is commonly not welcome and that which is not wanted, evidently an effrontery. (Samuel Johnson)

He who can take advice is sometimes superior to him who can give it. (Karl von Knebel)

We may give advice, but not the sense to use it. (François de la Rochefoucauld)

We give advice, but we cannot give the wisdom to profit by it. (François de la Rochefoucauld)

Your friends praise your abilities to the skies, submit to you in argument, and seem to have the greatest deference for you; but, though they may ask it, you never find them following your advice upon their own affairs; nor allowing you to manage your own, without thinking that you should follow theirs. Thus, in fact, they all think themselves wiser than you, whatever they may say. (Lord Melbourne)

Many receive advice, only the wise profit from it. (Publilius Syrus)

A word to the wise is infuriating. (Unknown source)

Giving advice to a fool is like giving medicine to a dead man. (Unknown source)

The only thing to do with good advice is to pass it on. It is never of any use to oneself. (Oscar Wilde)

Advice is the only commodity on the market where the supply always exceeds the demand. (Unknown source)

Most people, especially fools, don't listen to advice. Exceptional people do. This book aims to change that state of affairs!

What is the Value of Advice?

There is as much difference between the counsel that a friend giveth, and that a man giveth himself, as there is between the counsel of a friend and of a flatterer. For there is no such flatterer as is a man's self. (Francis Bacon)

No man is so foolish but he may sometimes give another good counsel, and no man so wise that he may not easily err if he takes no other counsel than his own. He that is taught only by himself has a fool for a master. (Ben Jonson)

Consult your friend on all things, especially on those which respect yourself. His counsel may then be useful where your own self-love might impair your judgment. (Seneca)

Advice compensates for your self-delusions.

Where there is no guidance, a people falls, but in an abundance of counselors there is safety. (Bible, Proverbs 11:14)

The counsel of many advisors can help to avoid serious mistakes.

I owe my success to having listened respectfully to the very best advice, and then going away and doing the exact opposite. (Gilbert K. Chesterton)

A good scare is worth more than good advice. (Horace)

It is only too easy to make suggestions and later try to escape the consequences of what we say. (Jawaharlal Nehru)

It is easy to give advice from a port of safety. (Johann Friedrich Von Schiller)

I have lived some thirty years on this planet, and I have yet to hear the first syllable of valuable or even earnest advice from my seniors. (Henry David Thoreau)

Give help rather than advice. (Marquis de Vauvenargues)

> To advise is easier than to help. (German proverb)
>
> I am glad that I paid so little attention to good advice; had I abided by it I might have been saved from some of my most valuable mistakes. (Gene Fowler)

Advice is worthless, or is inferior to actual help or to acting from a pressing need, or is ultimately harmful because it prevents you from making your own mistakes and learning from them.

> Good advice is beyond all price. (Proverb)

If advice is good, it's priceless.

> When we turn to one another for counsel we reduce the number of our enemies. (Kahlil Gibran)

Seeking advice builds good relationships, and can even repair them.

> These words dropped into my childish mind as if you should accidentally drop a ring into a deep well. I did not think of them much at the time, but there came a day in my life when the ring was fished up out of the well, good as new. (Harriet Beecher Stowe)

Advice can take time to have an effect.

Once again, we see that the wisdom contained in folk sayings and in quotations from famed authors is contradictory. I believe that a detailed analysis, as in Chapter 2, "What Advice Does for You," is more valuable than simple proverbs in trying to understand the benefits that are available.

Why Do People Seek or Heed Advice, or Why Don't They?

Most of us ask for advice when we know the answer but we want a different one. (Ivern Ball)

Consult. To seek another's approval of a course already decided on. (Ambrose Bierce)

Most people when they come to you for advice, come to have their own opinions strengthened, not corrected. (Henry Wheeler Shaw)

We ask advice but we mean approbation. (Charles Caleb Colton)

When we ask for advice, we are usually looking for an accomplice. (Marquis de la Grange)

No one wants advice, only corroboration. (John Steinbeck)

People are often looking just for moral support, not for new insights or alternative courses of action.

Advice is seldom welcome; and those who want it the most always like it the least. (Lord Chesterfield)

Advice is like castor oil, easy to give, but dreadful to take. (Josh Billings)

Taking advice is painful.

Only a fool learns from his own mistakes. The wise man

81

> learns from the mistakes of others. (Attributed to Otto von Bismarck)
>
> To profit from good advice requires more wisdom than to give it. (John Churton Collins)
>
> The way of a fool seems right to him, but a wise man listens to advice. (Bible, Proverbs 12:15)

Advice taking requires wisdom and benefits from knowledge of what has gone before.

Taken together, these sayings point out that often people are not so much looking to make better decisions but are in need of moral support, which is one of the benefits of advice that are discussed in Chapter 2, "What Advice Does for You." Taking advice can be painful and also requires wisdom. Hence the need for this book, which aims to make proactive advice seeking *normal* and to formulate best practices so that readers who seek out advice can build upon the knowledge of experienced practitioners, scholars, and folk wisdom.

We've now received all three scouting reports on the terrain of advice seeking. Combined with our earlier surveying, we can now embark on the journey whose goal is becoming proactive and skilled in seeking, getting, and using advice. Next, we will devise our own map of the terrain in the form of best practices, starting with *when* to seek advice.

Chapter 7: *When You Should Seek Advice*

Good advice-seeking opportunities range from picking what colleges or graduate schools to apply to, deciding on or changing a career, buying a house, repairing a strained relationship, and even to what unfamiliar beach to have your take-out dinner on before continuing on your way. Should we seek advice for everything? Is this desirable or even practical?

Surely you won't seek advice on simple issues like what clothes to wear on an unimportant day, whether to take an umbrella on your way to work, or why your cat doesn't seem to like its new cat food. But I believe that the range of issues that can benefit in practice are much larger than most people suspect. Let's consider a case not normally thought of as justifying deliberate advice seeking.

Eddie just entered the workforce and is having trouble living within his means because he's eating out too much. Eddie doesn't know how to organize his kitchen and food stocks so that he can buy varied, inexpensive, tasty food that's nutritious and not hard to prepare. Consulting the Web can help, but his tastes are not generic, he doesn't have a car so his access to groceries is limited, and he's overwhelmed by the variety of recipes and food advice on the Web, much of it trying to sell him something. Eddie could opt to do nothing special and so continue to live beyond his means (for a while), or he could just visit the nearest grocer and pick whatever he comes across.

Instead of that, however, Eddie could plan to seek advice. For example, he could identify three people who know about the subject or have had similar challenges recently, who are at least acquaintances who are friendly with him, and who perhaps live nearby. He could invite them out for coffee or just visit them and explain his needs and circumstances (what foods he likes, his feelings about leftovers, etc.) and then ask what they'd do or have done themselves. Their advice probably won't be incompatible, so he can combine ideas from all three advisors.

Since Eddie doesn't live at home anymore, he could also ask his mother (who doesn't live nearby), a female classmate and friend of his who seemed to always pay attention to healthy eating, and another male friend who finished school a year ago and has already had a year to face the same challenges Eddie faces. It turns out that these people enjoy being consulted. They point out some automobile-free shopping options that Eddie had no idea existed, recommend some simple recipes that worked well for them and that taste good as leftovers, and recommend some tricks—like buying edamame (Asian soybeans) at a local Oriental grocery on his way home, which he can heat in water in two minutes and use to complement whatever else he's having.

As a result of the process of consulting others, Eddie achieves better eating results and lives within his budget. He also enjoys his interactions with friends and family, and deepens his relationship with them. At the same time, one of the two friends asked Eddie for help when he was moving to a new apartment, and Eddie was happy to assist him. He even bragged about his new food success at work and shared tips with a college intern there who overheard him and had the same issues.

Scenarios for Advice Seeking

Is it worth going to the trouble of consulting others rather than just reacting to circumstances and changing nothing? I think it depends on how critical the need to solve the issue is—or at least to make some improvement in the situation. But it helps if you actually enjoy solving problems! If it's seen as drudgery to seek input from others, then maybe it's better to just react, improvise, or do nothing differently than you are doing.

Other life issues that could benefit from proactive advice seeking include:

1. I want to buy my first house. I'm newly married and intending to start a family in three years. What neighborhoods make sense for me?

2. Should I go to college or trade school? Where?

3. Should I go to college (or grad school) right away, or should I interrupt my studies for a year to do something else?

4. Should I send my five-year-old (the oldest of two) to public, private, or parochial school?

5. I finished my studies and need to find a job. How should I go about it? What jobs make sense for me?

6. I have an idea for starting my own small business. Is it worth taking the risk? How can I minimize my risks?

7. I'm a new schoolteacher of second-year Spanish. My classroom includes transfer students with no previous Spanish course, regular second-year students, and even students who speak Spanish at home with their parents. At whatever level I teach, I end up boring half the class. I can't deal with this anxiety and am thinking of quitting. What should I do?

8. My career isn't going anywhere. What other careers should I look at? Or should I stay in my career path and look for another job?

9. Should I leave the workforce and go back to school for more education?

10. I've been at a new job for six months and I like my boss, who is relying on me for an important new project. However, I was approached about an exciting new opportunity at another company, and I'm torn. What should I do?

11. I'm a married 25-year-old college grad, employed and satisfied with my chosen career. My husband and I want to have three children. When should we have the first? And the second?

12. I never had a dog while growing up. Should I get a dog for my family? Can my goals be met better with a different pet, or even no pet?

13. I don't know anything about marketing but would like to transfer to that department as a career move. What should I do to prepare?

Scoring a Scenario

Let's combine everything in this book up to now—the many real examples, personal and otherwise, scholarly research results, and folk wisdom expressed as proverbs, and especially Chapter 3, "28 Reasons for Not Seeking Advice"—and formulate 22 true–false questions that will help you discern when you should seek advice.

Each of the 22 questions (plus two subquestions) is followed by +True if judging the statement to be true adds 1 point to your score, or +False if judging the statement to be false adds 1 point. The maximum score is 22, since statements 7, 7a, and 7b together are designed to contribute at most 1 point. I'll use the word "mistake" as shorthand for either downright error or an inferior course of action. An online questionnaire with automatic scoring is available at AdviceIsForWinners.com under Tools. Let's look at the true–false questions.

1. **Others will suffer negative consequences if I do the wrong thing.**

+True. If you'll potentially harm others because of your mistakes or inaction, you have a duty to do your best, taking the initiatives that are called for.

2. **There is enough time to get advice before I take action.**

+True. I suspect that rarely is there not enough time. Even consulting a passerby on where to find a taxi doesn't consume much time.

3. **It matters a lot if I do the wrong thing.**

+True. However, even inconsequential issues can benefit from advice. For example, once I wanted to take my family to an Indian restaurant for a change. Rather than pick something off the Web, I consulted my co-workers of Indian origin for their varied recommendations. I learned something, enjoyed the dining, and my co-workers enjoyed making the recommendations.

4. **There may be totally different solutions or approaches to my problem that I'm not aware of.**

+True. For example, when deciding on a school for your children, someone might point out homeschooling as an option that you've never even considered. Or a young professional thinking about studying for an MBA might be directed toward an online program, which he or she never thought of due to his or her traditional, on-campus undergraduate experience.

> ### 5. Doing nothing is a possibility, and I'm not even sure what the "Do Something" options are.

+True. If it's viable to do nothing, then the work of getting and evaluating advice on positive actions could be doubly daunting. This suggests you really should get advice, because doing nothing could be too tempting.

> ### 6. Other people before me have often faced a similar problem.

+True. If it's a common problem, like where a young couple should buy their first home, it will be easy to find people who've been there and done that before.

> ### 7. I have already made up my mind what to do.

+False. If you already made up your mind, then don't bother getting advice, unless ...

> ### 7a. I've made up my mind, but I want to do a final "sanity check" to see if there's something I'm missing.

+True. A final check might offer a pleasant—or unpleasant but useful— surprise.

> ### 7b. I've made up my mind, but I want to get ongoing moral support or enlist allies.

+True. Even if you've decided on a course of action, you might need ongoing counsel or enthusiastic help, and you're more likely to get it if you've involved those advisors or helpers from the outset.

> ### 8. It's important to make my own mistakes so I can learn, because I'll have to do this again in the future. In other words, I need to practice.

+False. If practicing on your own, regardless of the consequences, matters most to you, then go for it. On the other hand, you can learn and practice your *advice seeking*, which is a skill that improves with practice, like any other.

9. **There is an obvious person to consult whom I already know or have easy access to.**

+True. If you already know some candidate advisors, all the more reason to take advantage of that happy circumstance.

10. **Both my advisor and I will enjoy the consultation and it may deepen the goodwill between us.**

+True. Regardless of the other factors, if you can improve on your relationship and enjoy the interaction, that's a good deal.

11. **Breaking new ground—devising a solution that nobody's thought of or done before—will be rewarded.**

+False. As pointed out by proverbs and common sense, if there's scope for innovation, sometimes it pays to ignore conventional wisdom and potential naysayers. Otherwise, this is no reason not to get advice.

12. **It's OK if I get contradictory advice. (For example, I could just pick one at random without getting stressed, or I could do nothing if that's a possibility.)**

+True. Probably few people will admit to being unnerved by contradictory advice. But it helps to make this explicit promise to oneself.

13. **I have too many other distractions that drain the energy I'd need to seek advice on this problem.**

+False. If you really have too much going on in your life unrelated to this issue, maybe it's not the right time to take action on this.

14. **The problem is routine: Several people in a similar situation would probably all benefit from the same solution.**

+False. If the problem is that routine, then the Web could be a good source of guidance rather than face-to-face advice. For example, if your computer is infected with a common virus, you can probably identify the problem and get a solution on the Web, because the solution is pretty much the same for everybody.

15. I am comfortable disregarding the advice that I get in the event that I feel that's the right course.

+True. If disregarding advice on what to do is problematic because it would come from people with authority over you, and they would feel offended, then maybe it's better not to get advice from them. However, the best thing would be *not* to seek advice on precise actions but rather on other aspects of the problem, as discussed in Chapter 2, "What Advice Does for You." For example, you can ask what dimensions of the problem you're not seeing, what criteria a good solution should be able to meet, or what are pitfalls to watch out for—without asking them to recommend actual solutions.

16. It bothers me if others think I'm weak because I'm seeking advice.

+False. As with another of the questions, rarely will people admit to being thought weak if they seek advice. But it helps to answer the question and be explicit with oneself.

17. My issue is an undertaking that will lead to a success or failure, and I'm concerned that my advisor will find out if I failed.

+False. Similarly, few people will confess to this fear, which they might not even be conscious of.

18. My issue is something shameful or embarrassing that I prefer to keep to myself.

+False. If true, books and the Web could still help, especially if the problem is routinely faced by others and isn't much complicated by individual circumstances. Alternatively, you could pay for professional advice or consult a religious counselor.

19. Getting advice would be easy and wouldn't make me or my advisor go to a lot of trouble.

+True. No obstacle in this case. But even if false, other factors can favor advice seeking.

20. Getting good advice is free, or I can afford it if it's not free.

+True. However, even if advice is costly, sometimes you can get free advice from others who see it as a cost of getting your business. For example, a lawyer might discuss your situation as an investment in getting signed up to carry out subsequent legal actions or formal fee-based services.

21. It's important to me to accomplish everything myself so that if I succeed there is no doubt as to who should get the credit.

+False. If this is truly important to you (but ask yourself why it should be), then consider asking privately for advice from people not otherwise involved in the issue. Better yet is to adopt President Ronald Reagan's attitude: "There is no limit to what a man can do or where he can go if he does not mind who gets the credit."

22. I strongly believe that everyone should try to solve problems by themselves before seeking help.

+False. If you strongly believe in this ethic, perhaps you should reconsider the basis for this belief. Artists and mathematicians are one model of heroic solitary problem solving, since these activities lend themselves to going it alone. But another model is that of leaders of organizations who deal with multifaceted issues, including people issues, for which they don't possess all the answers themselves. But every person is the CEO of his or her own life and of its multifaceted issues.

Some Scoring Examples

Let's apply the scoresheet to some of the stories told in this book, starting with my stopover on the Indiana lakefront to consume my take-out dinner while driving to Chicago from Pittsburgh. As I arrive at the parking area of the state park, I seek out someone to consult about the best place to go, for example, the officer at the entrance gate. My Indiana-beach example gives a score of 17/22 or 77%.

Next let's make up an example. I want to take my family to get ice cream at an ice cream shop in a couple of hours. I usually just get vanilla or chocolate chip, but I wonder if I'm missing out on an excellent experience by not trying some other flavor that an advisor could recommend. My ice-cream scoresheet yields a score of 13/22 or 59%.

Let's try a health example. Say that your wife or husband complains that you do not sleep well at night. You snore, gasp, and sometimes wake up temporarily, all of which disturbs your spouse's sleep, and this has been going on for some time. I've scored this one personally (it's happened to me!), giving a score of 19/22 or 86%.

These examples suggest that a borderline score is in the 70s. I wouldn't bother seeking advice about an ice cream outing, although I'd gladly listen to unsolicited advice. The snoring issue passes the threshold, and I did in fact visit a doctor, stay overnight at a sleep clinic, and was told I had sleep apnea, which I had never heard of but learned is fairly common and luckily disappears after losing weight.

On the question of when to seek advice, this chapter has argued for the answer: *Often, but think it through*. Building on Chapter 3, "28 Reasons for Not Seeking Advice," it's possible to design a questionnaire and score the results to give an idea of the potential scope for advice seeking. I don't encourage readers to pick a pass/fail threshold but to answer the questions on some realistic cases and explicitly consider one's goals and circumstances, all in the service of becoming more skilled in this art.

This chapter has been our first contribution to a map of the advice-seeking terrain. Upon deciding that external advice is worthwhile, the next step is to realize who can give it, which of course depends on your situation. We turn to that in the next chapter.

Chapter 8: Who is a Good Advisor?

Once I was considering a business idea that used technology to analyze data in various subjects and then deliver insights to users over the Web. I was seeking reactions to the idea, so I wrote to a fellow who had experience that was relevant to potential uses of the technology. I had had lunch with him a year before, when he was developing his own business ideas and was looking for feedback and networking contacts. We agreed to meet once again, so I showed up with a laptop bag ready to demonstrate the idea.

I was interested in how his own project was doing, so we spent the first 30 minutes talking about his progress and challenges. Then we switched gears, and I gave a very brief verbal introduction to the idea and why it might be new and interesting. After a couple of minutes, this fellow said that he "got it" and began talking continuously for 5 to 10 minutes, speaking about matters that in his mind were related. After this time, during which I said nothing, he paused and asked if that had helped. I replied, "No" and then decided merely to ask if he could recommend someone with expertise in the area of my idea to whom I could speak. I decided at that point that doing a restart, getting out my laptop, and starting to talk again, would not be fruitful. We chatted a couple of minutes more and then I thanked him for his remarks and said goodbye. What went wrong here?

An obvious lesson is that not all attempts are fruitful, but then I already knew that. A second lesson, which I already felt intuitively but which this visit imprinted on me, is that good advisors must be good listeners, as emphasized by Covey in his *7 Habits* book. The best advice requires understanding others' circumstances, which in turn requires time, patience, and listening. A third lesson is that poor listeners might be poor because of personality reasons or because they are distracted by their own personal, professional, or business matters. (Should you seek marital advice from someone going through an ugly divorce?) In short, seek out good listeners who have stable personal situations, and don't be disappointed if not every session goes well. Recall the proverb in Chapter 6, "What Proverbs Say," taken from an Aesop fable: "Never trust the advice of a man in difficulties."

In *The Wise Advisor*, written for professional consultants or advice givers, in the second chapter, "Know Your Client," J. W. Salacuse says this:

> Good advice must always meet your client's needs and circumstances, and your client is usually the best source of that information. A financial counselor cannot create an effective estate plan for a widow without knowing her income, expenses, lifestyle, family relationships, and assets. An auto salesman cannot really advise a customer on a car without knowing the customer's family size, driving habits, and commuting needs. [...]
>
> A second reason for knowing your client concerns the advising process itself—the way you go about giving advice. The effective advisor shapes the advising process to fit the client's abilities and background. To do that, you must know the client.

Salacuse warns advisors not to jump too readily to solutions based on superficially similar cases seen before: "The advisor comes to see a client as a specific type of problem, rather than as a unique individual in a particular circumstance with a special set of needs, resources, and desires. ... It is important to remember that each client is unique."

Qualities of Good Advisors

To figure out who makes a good advisor in the general case, we should identify the qualities they need to have so that we can determine if an advisor possesses them. Building upon the previous chapters, we can say that good advisors should be:

1. **Experienced.** In the case of multiple advisors, it's ideal if each one has experience that differs from the experience of the others. Recall the proverb: He that has no children brings them up well.

2. **Discreet.** Recall the proverb: "Never give advice in a crowd."

3. **Good listeners.** Besides the quoted passages from *The Wise Advisor*, recall the passage from *The 7 Habits of Highly Effective People*: "Although it's risky and hard, seek first to understand, or diagnose before you prescribe, is a correct principle manifest in many areas of life."

4. **Serene or unburdened.** Recall the proverb: "Never trust the advice of a man in difficulties."

5. **Able to teach, convey reasons and principles, and motivate.** Recall the writing of Phillips Brooks:

> The best advisers, helpers and friends, always are not those who tell us how to act in special cases, but who give us, out of themselves, the ardent spirit and desire to act right, and leave us then, even through many blunders, to find out what our own form of right action is.

In my experience, *doers* are not always the best teachers, because to teach or advise—beyond just telling what they'd do or have done in the past—advisors need an ability to *generalize* so that their experiences become applicable to the situations of others. Consider an extreme analogy: The mongoose knows how to defeat many snakes, but can't teach us to do the same. If the needed advice is just a specific solution or action, that may be OK, but even so, knowing *why* helps one to proceed with confidence.

6. **Humble, in the sense of not taking offense if you don't follow their advice.** Recall the earlier citation of Hannah Whitall Smith: "The true secret of giving advice is, after you have honestly given it, to be perfectly indifferent whether it is taken or not, and never persist in trying to set people right."

7. **Someone who cares about you.** Recall the proverb: "Write down the advice of him who loves you, though you like it not at present."

8. **Social, in the sense of being able to connect to people, ideas, and sources outside of themselves.** Such people either have a wide network of friends, acquaintances, and social-media contacts that they can make matches with, or they are well read and so can supply links to the world of written advice and knowledge.

It's worth highlighting one of these qualities, which was absent from the protagonist of the story that opens this chapter, and which is stressed by Covey's *7 Habits*: Being a good listener. Many cases that cry out for advice are complicated, meaning that one's situation and individuality strongly influence the right course of action. If an advisor doesn't know you well or doesn't listen first and *then* offer advice, how does such one-size-fits-all advice differ from the one-way interactions of reading a book or searching the Web? If a potential advisor does not first listen to you, then you should discount the advice, not by ignoring it, but by thinking of it as you would think of advice you got out of a book. For example, you could still learn about general principles and gain general awareness of the issues and courses of action, as well as pointers to other relevant people or sources. Better yet would be to proactively structure the advisory session by "coaching" the advisor into listening to you first.

Matching Advisor Qualities to Needs

To answer this chapter's question of who's a good advisor, let's match the eight advisor qualities we just looked at with the advice seeker's needs. First, let's revisit the framework from Chapter 2, "What Advice Does for You:"

1. **Solutions**—An advisor provides information that is used to generate solutions to problems, especially how-to information.

2. **Pointers**—An advisor gives pointers to individuals, locations, or documents that have relevant expertise. (The cited article calls this "meta-knowledge.")

3. **Framing**—The advisor points out aspects of the problem that may not be recognized, helping to change how one frames the problem and the criteria that a solution should meet.

4. **Validation**—An advisor provides confidence that one's approach or solution is a good one.

5. **Legitimation**—A respected advisor becomes a source of credibility that helps one move toward a solution.

6. **Engagement**—An agreeable (pleasurable) experience that provides memorable moments and may help build social capital, which results from establishing human bonds of goodwill and trust that can be deepened and called upon over time.

Now let's make a table of advisor qualities (the *rows*) and advice seeker's needs (the *columns*). I have excluded *engagement* from the columns because it is a side benefit of advice seeking, not its driver. Recall that we are viewing advice seeking as driven by a problem to be solved. If engagement is the sole goal, then that's really pure networking, not advice seeking.

	SOLUTIONS	POINTERS	FRAMING	VALIDATION	LEGITIMATION
EXPERIENCED		⇨	⇩		⇩
DISCREET		⇨			
LISTENS		⇨			
SERENE		⇨			
TEACHES					
HUMBLE	⇩	⇨	⇨		
CARES				⇩	
SOCIAL		⇩			

Clearly, one desires an advisor who has all eight qualities and is able to supply all five benefits. If you find such a person, please contact this author right away with an introduction! If not, don't despair, because Earth has few such inhabitants.

Let's use the table to formulate some rules of the form *If you need A, seek someone who's B*. The entry A,B in the table will be marked with a ⇩ to show that the starting point is the need at the top of that column.

97

- If you need solutions, seek someone humble.
- If you need pointers, seek someone social.
- If you need help framing the problem, seek someone experienced.
- If you need validation, seek someone who cares about you.
- If you seek legitimation, seek someone experienced.

We can formulate another type of rule: *If an advisor isn't B, then seek advice of type A.* Those table entries are marked with a right arrow to show that the starting point is the advisor quality on that row at the table's left.

- If someone is inexperienced, indiscreet, doesn't listen well, or is burdened, then seek pointers.
- If someone isn't humble, then seek pointers or framing, but not solutions, unless you know you'll follow their advice, or unless you're not troubled if you don't and they resent it.

To illustrate the last two, here are a couple of archetypes that require special handling:

- **The non-humble "tyrant."** A domineering or self-proud individual who has power over you. Don't ask them for solutions, or open the door to solutions by asking for open-ended advice. Instead, specifically ask for help with pointers or aspects of your problem, making it clear that you intend to devise a solution with the best input you can find from them and others. This is especially good if the individual is in a position to obstruct your approach; better to engage their participation early.
- **The "egocentric" poor listener.** Someone is not a good listener, either by personality or due to his own burdens, but is otherwise an expert in your subject matter or is social in the sense of having a wide social network—at least better than yours. In that case, it's better not to force them to listen to you. Instead, briefly state your problem and ask for pointers or other people you could speak with.

In some cases, one can get more specific about further qualities that advisors should have. For example, the book *Taking Advice: How Leaders Get Good Counsel and Use It Wisely* by Dan Ciampa, deals with leaders—CEOs or other senior executive in large organizations—who are undertaking complex changes such as taking over as the new leader, or redirecting their current organization toward new goals. Ciampa argues that such leaders should have a well-balanced advice network that addresses strategic, operational, political, and personal issues. Political issues deal with "interpersonal relationships, internal competition for influence, and the interplay of coalitions and interest groups" within an organization, whereas personal issues deal with the leader's emotions, stress, and composure.

This chapter is our second contribution to mapping out the terrain of advice seeking, after the previous chapter considered the issue of when getting advice is justified. Now that we know who can be a good advisor, we'll look next at good practices for actually getting one or several.

Chapter 9: How to Get an Advisor

As Chairman of the company I had co-founded years earlier, I received a LinkedIn invitation from an employee whom I didn't know. The employee invited me to combine our professional networks, the equivalent of "friending" someone on the well-known Facebook social website. This employee's desk wasn't far from mine. I replied in my usual way, saying that I would be glad to combine our networks but that I never took that step unless I knew the individual. I wrote that I would be happy to spend some time getting to know him and vice versa, and I invited him to drop by my office sometime to chat. He never acted on this suggestion nor replied to my email.

What was wrong with this outcome? The chairman of his employer had shown a willingness, indeed an interest, in getting to know him, but the young employee did not rouse himself to drop by an office that was a minute away. Embarrassment? Shyness? Perhaps, but in any case, a wasted opportunity.

A second example: I received the following polite email from a young lady—let's call her Elizabeth Adams—whom I did not remember but who apparently had met me during an event associated with a nonprofit that my daughter volunteered for during her high school years:

> Dear Dr. Valdes-Perez,
>
> As a reminder to who I am, I met you through your daughter ... when I volunteered with her at the [nonprofit] years ago. I am now looking for a change and I was wondering if

Vivisimo would be a fit. Although I have a degree in Psychology and a certification with infants, tots, and toddlers, I have been using my computer skills my whole life. My updated resume explains how my job now requires my computer skills. Other teachers have asked me to type up pictures or letters for them as well. My boss has complimented me on my use of the computer with my new lesson plans. I was wondering if I could use basic computer skills at Vivisimo, or if you had any ideas for me. I use many sites online and I type up documents as well. People ask me to look at their computers and help them. I go to the library and help one co-worker send some emails and I have helped others buy things. I try to troubleshoot issues for people as well.

I am looking forward to hearing if you have any suggestions for me.

Thanks again.

I emailed this reply:

Dear Ms. Adams,

Thank you for your interest in Vivisimo. I believe that the only openings now are for technical positions requiring a computer science or IT [information technology] background, so I'm afraid that Vivisimo may not be a fit, but I'll let our human resources staff decide that, since I may be misinformed. If you'll send me your resume directly, I promise to take a look and see if anything occurs to me that may be of value to you.

After giving it some more thought and consulting internally, I also sent this message:

> Hi Elizabeth, I've not had any great insights into openings I could connect you with. However, if you'd like someone to talk with, to help you think through your career and options, I'd be happy to have a conversation with you. Our offices are on the corner of Forbes and Murray in Squirrel Hill.

I soon received this reply:

> Thanks for thinking of me. I am going away soon and I will think about what I would like to discuss with you and get back to you. Thanks again! Elizabeth

But there was no subsequent follow-up. This was an opportunity for a young person to get some career advice, or at least get a sounding board for her ideas. Moreover, if during an in-person meeting she made a good impression with her sincerity and earnestness, she could have gained someone to call on in the future. Why was this opportunity wasted? One can never know for sure, but I suspect that shyness was not the cause, because Elizabeth was not shy about writing in the first place. Instead, I surmise that Elizabeth was looking not for guidance, but for a solution, that is, a job. Since I was not in a position at that time to point her at a specific job, maybe Elizabeth didn't feel like investing her time or emotional energy.

My suggestion to any young—or not so young—person is to answer somewhat like this:

> Thank you so much for kindly offering your time and help. I am about to go on a trip but will be back on ... Please indicate a couple of times that I could pay a visit, at your convenience. I work during X to Y on weekdays, and it's not easy for me to get away, but I'll do what I can, since I would really like to get your career advice.

As a third example of how *not* to get an advisor: An experienced person (I'll call him "Larry") whom I had dealt with in the past wrote me out of the blue as shown in the following exchanges.

> *[Wednesday]*—Raul, Happy New Year! It's been a while. I hope all is well. I'd like your advice. We're raising money to expand operations, and I'm uncertain about whether I want to stay on or cash out. I'd like to know what it's been like for you since your investors came on board. This was a great experience for me to build a company, and I'm not sure I'll have the same experience with VCs [venture capitalists, i.e., professional investors] running the company. If you have some time, I'll buy you lunch.

I was happy to hear from Larry and had always liked him, so I replied with interest and we had the subsequent exchanges.

> *[Same Wednesday]*—Hi Larry, happy new year to you as well. I'd be happy to serve as a sounding board. Please suggest a few dates for lunch.
>
> *[Friday, two days later]*—Larry, are you there?
>
> *[Sunday, two days later]*—Hey Raul, Sorry I took so long to respond. I'll be in Pittsburgh this Wednesday the 12th. If you're available anytime between noon and 2 pm let me know. If not, no worries, we can do it some other time.
>
> *[Sunday, an hour later]*—Larry, unfortunately Wednesday is a bad day for lunch. If you'd like to meet for dinner instead, that will work. Otherwise, I'll wait to hear from you about new dates that you'll be in town.
>
> *[Sunday, an hour later]*—Raul, Sorry, can't make dinner. I'm in Pittsburgh on the 19th. So far, my only meeting is 9-11 am. I hope this works for you.

> *[Monday]*—Larry, lunch on the 19th [nine days later] would work, as of this writing.
>
> *[Wednesday at 10:45am, nine days later]*—Raul, Are we on for lunch today?
>
> *[Wednesday* after *lunch]*—Larry, sorry, I never heard from you that you wanted to proceed.

No further exchanges happened after that. What went wrong? The potential advice giver (me, in this case) is left with the impression that Larry the advice seeker isn't very serious, or doesn't much care one way or the other about the meeting actually taking place. Absent a substantial reservoir of accumulated goodwill, the flippancy of this exchange lessens the chances of our resuming the interaction along similar lines in the future.

Principles for Approaching Advisors

The following small number of commonsense principles would prevent any of the three above situations from happening:

1. **Waste not, want not.** Don't squander small opportunities to "build relationships" (as is said in the business world), which really means to establish human bonds of goodwill and trust that can be deepened and called upon over time. Sociologists call this social capital.

2. **Realize that advice consists of more than just immediate solutions.** As discussed in Chapter 2, "What Advice Does for You," advice can also contribute pointers, framing, validation, legitimation, and engagement. Don't spurn these other benefits, which may also lead indirectly to solutions.

3. **The petitioner defers to the petitioned.** The advice seeker must yield to the advisor's convenience, regardless of comparative stature, unless the seeker is king, queen, or president of the country. This deference is reflected not only in the logistics of meetings but in language, promptness of replies, and other little courtesies.

With regard to the last principle above, I recall the 2010 British historical-drama film *The King's Speech*, in which King George VI goes to see a speech therapist—an Australian, not even an Englishman—for help with his severe stuttering, which hinders him as he tries to inspire his subjects for imminent war with Nazi Germany. Despite the uneven stature of king versus overseas subject, King George treats the therapist with real deference, as befits their roles of petitioner and the petitioned expert consultant.

Ways to Get Advice

So far in this chapter we've seen three examples of how *not* to get an advisor and looked at several commonsense principles that the stories violated. Previous chapters have looked at what advice consists of and the qualities that good advisors have, which sometimes depends on the type of advice that is needed. Let's now examine good practices for *getting* advice.

As shown on the left side of Figure 1, the starting point is your *problem* and your *reputation*. A problem is any issue on which you seek advice. Reputation refers to the impressions of you that potential advisors will form based on (1) any previous exchanges with them, (2) your public persona on the Web or other social media, and (3) the friends and acquaintances that you have in common with your potential advisors. Unless you're famous or occupy a prestigious or respectable position (Supreme Court Justice, Headmaster, clergy, prominent business person, etc.), these make up your reputation.

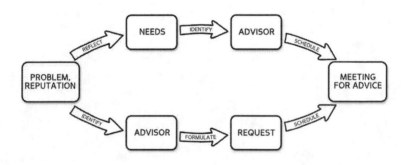

Figure 1

It's important to point out that your reputation increasingly will depend on your public profile and postings as revealed on the Web and social media.

A story here is worthwhile: While driving in New England on vacation one summer, we found ourselves in Providence, Rhode Island, and decided to take in a tour of Brown University. Our student tour guide mentioned that a Brown professor had an unusual way of interacting with his class: The professor would project students' Facebook pages on a screen as a way of calling on them. Some young people I've told this story to were mortified, considering this an invasion of privacy, which is odd since these highly public profiles are entirely constructed by the users themselves for anyone to check out. The professor's point was that these public profiles are fair game as a basis for your reputation, so get used to it: Others will be checking out your profile and making their own judgments, unknown to you.

Figure 1 shows two different paths for getting an advisor. One path is needs-driven; on that path you must figure out what you need and then approach someone who could help with that need. A second path is advisor-driven in the sense that you identify someone with a willing ear who has some relevant experience or expertise and figure out what needs they could help with.

Let's consider the needs-driven path first. Recall that Chapter 2, "What Advice Does for You," lists six benefits that we can shorten to these:

1. Solutions, or how to find solutions

2. Pointers for follow-up investigation

3. Framing of problem aspects, e.g., what am I not seeing?

4. Validation

5. Legitimation

6. Engagement

Try to identify which benefits you're seeking and approach individuals best suited to fulfill them. (If your needs are "all of the above," then you're really following the second, advisor-driven path, which we'll get to shortly.) Since our intent is not to set up a complex design problem akin to designing an oil refinery, let's instead come up with simple rules of thumb for advisors for each need.

1. *Solutions* → people knowledgeable or experienced in your problem area.

2. *Pointers* → generally knowledgeable people who know at least a little about your problem area but know more about neighboring areas, or have a wide circle of experience and acquaintances.

3. *Framing*→ imaginative people who are generally good problem solvers.

4. *Validation*→ people knowledgeable or experienced in your problem area.

5. *Legitimation* → people with accomplishments in your problem area or a neighboring area.

6. *Engagement* → people you'd like to have a better acquaintance with.

The patterns common to these six rules of thumb are (1) experience or knowledge specific to your problem, (2) a wide knowledge of neighboring subjects, and (3) acquaintance with other relevant people.

The next step is to filter out canned, one-size-fits-all sources of advice. Can you solve your problem just by consulting books or the Web? That is, is your problem generic and do its solutions depend so little on your individual circumstances that published guides are good enough? If so, try those first. Otherwise, armed with a conscious awareness of your specific needs (still on the diagram's upper path), you need to identify potential advisors. Some possibilities:

- Relative

- Friend

- Friendly acquaintance

- Friend/acquaintance of a friend/acquaintance

- Electronic acquaintance (Facebook friend, LinkedIn connection, etc.)

- Stranger (i.e., someone who you can't get an introduction to but have to approach "cold").

How can you identify friends-of-friends or strangers? Luckily, Web services like LinkedIn are great at searching for professional expertise. Type in a topic and optionally a zip code, and the service will return people's profiles and whether you are linked to them directly, or via one step—still useful in my experience—or two steps, meaning the friend/acquaintance of a friend/acquaintance of a friend/acquaintance, which I've found to be too distant to have much usefulness. LinkedIn lets you ask your links for introductions using their service, or you can contact your links directly outside of LinkedIn to ask for the introduction, which is my preference.

Identifying the right strangers is trickier. You'll need help from some of these: (1) a strong reputation; (2) something in common with the stranger; (3) an interesting and persuasive story to approach with. Let's say that I'm a recent college graduate, I want to break into the finance industry, and I am open to relocating. I could go on LinkedIn and search for members who mention "finance" or "financial" in their profiles and who are fellow alumni of my college. But that might not be enough to get replies. If, however, you served in student government, were in a fraternity or sorority, played on the volleyball team, or belonged to a club, you could add those topics to your search terms and identify strangers that you have two things in common with: alma mater and interests.

I tried the following experiment on LinkedIn. There are 38,950 members who mention "Tufts" (e.g., Tufts University) as their school. Requiring a mention of the phrase "student senate" narrows that down to 74. Further requiring mention of "finance" OR "financial" gives 17 members, who live all across the country. Would a fellow alum who also served in Student Senate and works in an industry you want to break into, agree to offer some advice? Maybe. It will help if your "reputation" (public profile on LinkedIn, in this case) is good and your approach is done earnestly and tastefully. Not everyone will reply, but so what?

What if the problem does not involve specific professional expertise but is rather one of life's issues that nobody would insert in a public profile? In that case, you can meet with a relative or friend, pose your problem and explain your need, and ask them for recommendations of whom to speak with.

Now let's look at the advisor-driven path in the diagram. Given the ear of a knowledgeable, experienced, or well-connected person, figure out what needs that advisor can best supply and focus the discussion on that need. Good advisors will want to know how they can help, so you should plan for that, even if the fallback need is as fuzzy as: Here's *my situation and what I'm thinking of doing. Do you have any thoughts or recommendations, or do you see aspects that I'm not seeing?*

In the course of writing this book I followed the advisor-driven approach many times. In one case, over dinner at my home with a longtime friend, I told her about my writing this book, mentioned how I had learned something new every time I discussed this project with someone, and asked her who among her social circle was the "wisest person about the full spectrum of human relations" that she knew. I wrote to the person she recommended, an attorney now heading up a local non-profit, paid him a visit, took him to lunch, enjoyed an interesting conversation, and added remarks to Chapter 1 on how this book's goal differs from the many books that are written on business networking, a question that he thought would arise. I took a similar approach with others, and this book is filled with their suggestions, including a number of reasons why people often don't seek advice (see Chapter 3, "28 Reasons for Not Seeking Advice") that hadn't occurred to me.

In summary, there are principles that govern seeking out an advisor: (1) don't waste small opportunities to engage with potential advisors or mentors, (2) realize that advisors sometimes cannot provide direct solutions but they can provide other advisory benefits, and (3) defer completely to their convenience while being at your most courteous, even if you are President of the United States or Queen of England. Starting with your problem and your reputation, you can either find individuals to help with certain needs, or take advantage of having fortunate access to relevant people and ask for the thoughts or help that they are best able to provide. Your social network consists of relatives, friends, and friends-of-friends, and even strangers if you approach them with the right humility, deference, ambition, clarity, and taste.

As we finish this chapter, our terrain map of best practices is halfway done. Now we can recognize when it's worthwhile to seek advice, who the good advisors are, and how to find them. We'll look next at how to set up the process after the advisors have been identified.

Chapter 10: How to Set Up an Advice Process

The English philosopher and mathematician Alfred North Whitehead wrote the following in his 1911 book *An Introduction to Mathematics*:

> It is a profoundly erroneous truism, repeated by all copy-books and by eminent people when they are making speeches, that we should cultivate the habit of thinking of what we are doing. The precise opposite is the case. Civilization advances by extending the number of important operations which we can perform without thinking about them. Operations of thought are like cavalry charges in a battle—they are strictly limited in number, they require fresh horses, and must only be made at decisive moments.

Although his first two sentences are phrased provocatively, Whitehead reasonably points out that we can't be thinking all the time. Thinking is exhausting, it interrupts the flow of actions, and it imposes burdens of creativity that are impossible to meet regularly. That's why we have cookbooks, so that we don't need to invent recipes at every meal. We can just apply well-tested solutions developed by others and don't have to innovate. If a certain "operation"—Whitehead's term—can be made routine, then people can spend their time on other activities that have not yet become routine.

The World Wide Web offers countless examples of new operations that can be performed without much thought. My favorite is mapping websites like Mapquest or Google Maps. Plotting a driving path from point A to B is now completely routine and needs little thought, except in cases where several alternate routes are presented, inviting one's evaluation of which is best. Therefore, civilization has advanced, according to Whitehead.

This book's goal is to make advice seeking frequent, routine, and fruitful. By thinking through what is involved from beginning to end, finding patterns in numerous examples both successful and failed, and combining these with insights from folk wisdom and earlier writings, we should be able to make the process more cookbookish and less reliant on creativity, which otherwise would be needed if every case were one-of-a-kind.

Let's examine some advice searches in detail, both successful and unsuccessful, from my own affairs and from that of others. After these illustrations, and building on the prior chapters, let's try to come close to a recipe that can guide many situations.

Recruiting a Vice President

The first example relates to Vivisimo. About nine years after Vivisimo's founding, it was decided to recruit a vice president of engineering. My two technical co-founders had served as de facto VPs of engineering, although without holding that job title, and after early growth we brought on a director of engineering. The time had come to bring on a VP who had similar experience with a software company before, had managed a sizable group of software engineers, and had delivered a software product through multiple development-and-release cycles, which is more complicated than just getting an initial product to market.

At that point I was Chairman of Vivisimo and was not involved in the day-to-day operations, so rather than rely on job postings or an external recruiter, I volunteered for the task of identifying good candidates and getting them interested. Clearly the task called for getting good advice about who the right candidates were.

I came up with the following plan: I would start with a handful of senior engineering people who I had come across at local events or who had been professional references for earlier job candidates. I had made sure to take the time in the past to let those references know the successful outcome of people they had recommended, which they tended to remember and appreciate. So I contacted a few people by phone, stating that we were looking to hire a VP of engineering and that I'd appreciate a dialogue with them over lunch or coffee in order to get their thoughts and recommendations. Ordinary mortals have lunch everyday anyway, and I would offer to meet them at a place of their choice, which makes it easy to say yes.

With each person I met, after we'd updated one another on our respective activities, I posed the same problem: "We are looking to hire our first-ever VP of engineering, the opportunity is a good one, the general profile we're looking for is such-and-such, we want to get the best person in all of Pittsburgh, and we don't care if the person is looking for a job or not right now. Who do you recommend that I go and meet to tell about the opportunity?" After hearing their thoughts on suitable candidates, I would ask them to rank the individuals if they could, all the while taking notes. Then, as appropriate, I would ask each person if he or she also should be considered a fit for our needs. Then I would pay for whatever was consumed, thank them for their time and thoughts, and remind them to contact me if there was something I could do for them sometime. More often than not, I would contact and meet with the people they had recommended.

This process proved interesting and fruitful, and those I met with found it flattering to be approached like this. One person I met with, whom I had never met before this process, sent this email the day after our initial meeting:

> Thank you for meeting yesterday. It was a pleasure to hear of the progress you've made and the challenges ahead. Let me know what additional discussion you or your team would like to have. I must admit I was flattered, and a bit surprised (pleasantly so) at your interest in my career plans. In parallel with our continued discussions, I will also spend some time in the next few days digging through my virtual rolodex to see if there are any other names that come to mind.

It turned out that he became our senior VP of engineering and was an outstanding choice. Of course, I informed "Raquel," the person who first mentioned him to me nearly three months earlier, with this email:

> Hi Raquel, I wanted to close the loop on this ... he accepted our offer to join us as VP Engineering and starts in February. Thanks again for your input to this successful process.

Let's now look at another personal example that was not successful despite my best and most careful efforts and see what could have been done differently.

Getting Legal Advice

At one point, as I was considering my personal financial situation and the general issues of inheritance, mortality, and taxes, I became intrigued by the possibility of setting up a legal instrument that receives ownership of some assets and deals with the legal and tax consequences as an entity, not as an individual human taxpayer. I knew little about such matters, but I did read a lengthy article or two that prompted me to take some steps. I contacted an accountant and a lawyer, two individuals that my employer had a good business relationship with, and asked for their recommendation of a local specialist attorney. Surprisingly, both individuals independently recommended the same person, whom I proceeded to contact and will call "Nathan" here for our purposes. I also got other recommendations that I didn't investigate because the overlapping recommendation from an accountant and a lawyer seemed to be good enough.

During our initial phone call, Nathan listened to my explanation of what I was looking for and then gave me an overview of how such entities work generally. Then he sent me a lengthy article explaining the details of one particular type of entity, since there are many types. I read the article, which was complicated and written more for experts than for someone like me. I also mentioned the idea confidentially to several people I was close with but who knew little more, or even less, about the matter than I did.

Since there was no pressing need to make any decision, I let it all sink in over a period of months before I finally decided to move forward. I set up an in-person meeting with Nathan at which I got to know him better as an individual and explored with him the possibility that there were people we knew in common. But we mostly discussed technical details, including the many questions I had thought about and prepared for our meeting. For example, I asked Nathan what would happen if I later changed my mind; was this an irreversible action or could I undo my actions? This and a subsequent meeting both went well, so I asked Nathan for references to people like me whose needs he had served successfully. I told him that if this wasn't possible due to attorney–client privilege, then I would understand (but I would have privately considered it a demerit in terms of proceeding with him). After consulting his clients, Nathan said that two of them would be happy to speak with me. After checking their profiles on a business networking site

(LinkedIn) and speaking with them about their experiences with Nathan, I was confident that I had done enough "due diligence" (background checking) to be able to proceed with setting up the entity through Nathan. And so I did.

Let's review my advice seeking procedures to this point:

- I consulted two trusted, separate business service providers (legal and accounting) for their recommended attorney, and they both pointed me to Nathan (I also consulted others, who gave me other names besides Nathan).
- I talked with Nathan over the phone and read the materials that he made available.
- I let it all sink in over a period of months and discussed it informally with some peers (but not experts), until I was comfortable proceeding.
- I met with Nathan at length, twice, and asked him many questions. Among my questions was what happened if I later changed my mind, such that I wanted to undo what I had done by removing the assets from the entity. Nathan handled my questions well.
- I talked with the two client references that Nathan had supplied, of people whose needs were similar to mine.

I was satisfied that I had done enough careful evaluation.

After setting up the entity, I started to have misgivings. I took some of my concerns to Nathan, but my doubts were not removed. I then took a step which, in hindsight, was missing from my careful "due diligence."—I decided to seek other legal opinions. I had done reading, asked for references and talked with them, and let all the complicated information sink in, but I had never gotten a second opinion on the legal approach that I was following. Of course, getting a second opinion is a known recommended practice for complicated medical conditions, but it didn't occur to me to transfer this practice to my case dealing with complicated legal matters.

At that point, I asked two other trusted business and social acquaintances for recommendations of attorneys to get a second opinion on the entity that I had set up. I was in for a shock: Both these new attorneys were of the opinion that Nathan's approach had been "pushing the envelope" and would not work in terms of its tax implications if it underwent close analysis. I now had new information that I lacked before. Had I been armed with this information, I wouldn't have gone down the path I took with Nathan, regardless of who was right, since financial and/or tax innovation doesn't fit my temperament. As it turned out, I undid the entity. All in all, I wasted effort and money on legal bills, and I endured aggravation by not doing enough to answer the question: "What can go wrong?" I had asked myself as well as Nathan that question, but never asked any third party.

The lesson from this detailed example is that things can go awry despite one's best efforts to cover all the bases. I had followed very similar processes in business tasks such as selecting an investment banker and an outside executive recruiter while at Vivisimo, with good outcomes. The difference here is that I was selecting not just a person, but a person and an approach, so I needed to do two evaluations and not just evaluate the person. Getting a second or third opinion on complicated subjects from knowledgeable practitioners is worth the trouble and expense.

Testing an Idea

Let's explore a third example. I was once contacted by a budding entrepreneur and his partner who had a sports-related idea and had built a prototype. The idea wasn't related to technology, but the individual approached me because I had met him years ago, he had lent me a hand in the past, I had dabbled in sports-related technology myself, and probably because of my own experiences as an entrepreneur. He and his partner were looking for any thoughts I could offer, and I was happy to make some suggestions about ways to get introductions and what the real competition for their idea would be, since they had two superficially similar—but in reality very different—markets for their product.

Everything went fine except for a couple of items that were not ingratiating. First, one of them asked whether I had graduated from such-and-such college, which puzzled me until he pointed out a memento that I had on my desk. I explained that I had been given the memento as a gift for some service that I provided to that college. Now it would have been better if they had prepared for the meeting by taking a few seconds to look up my background on the Web, or even easier, on a professional social-networking site like LinkedIn, which people use to publicize their backgrounds and interests. Doing that would have shown that they cared enough to prepare for the meeting. Second, they stated that they were rushed because of a subsequent meeting for a similar purpose, and were doing the rounds. Personally, I would have said only that they were expected elsewhere at a certain time, rather than imply that their sounding board (me) was just another stop in their route for the day. The principle is the same as the principle of knowing something about the person from whom you're seeking advice: Show your potential advisor that he or she is important to you, which contributes to successful human relations in business as well as in friendship and romance.

This last story isn't uncommon. Shortly afterwards, I had dinner with a former client, "Harry," whom I had always liked and whose company I enjoyed. He told me about his financial involvement with a technology start-up and asked if I would have a conversation with the founder/entrepreneur "Samantha," since I had some expertise that was relevant to the company's goals. I was happy to perform this favor, so we set up a phone call. The call started awkwardly with Samantha asking me questions about my background that showed she had done no preparation; her questions could have been answered in seconds with a search on the Web or on LinkedIn. Also, Samantha began the one-on-one call on speakerphone, which always has a mechanical sound to it, until I asked her to remove the speaker so I could hear better. Speaking with someone for the first time by speakerphone is like shaking hands with a new acquaintance without removing your gloves. I ended up fulfilling the favor to Harry on this call and with several follow-ups. However, had Harry not been involved, I probably would not have helped Samantha and followed up as proactively as I did.

Setting Up an Encounter

We've seen several stories of successful, failed, and middling advisory sessions. Before trying to formulate a recipe, let's look at what good advisors *themselves* look for in similar sessions. In the chapter "Know Your Client" in his book *The Wise Advisor*, J. W. Salacuse encourages professional advisors/consultants to extract key pieces of information from the client advice seeker. He writes:

> A client is therefore like a traveler. Any advisor, whether a doctor or lawyer, consulting engineer or financial planner, needs to get answers to the three traveler's questions to really know the client: (1) Where have you been?; (2) Where are you now?; and (3) Where do you want to go?

In the chapter "Agree on Your Role," Salacuse explains as follows:

A first step for the advisor is to determine what role the prospective client sees for the advisor. The advisor often begins this phase simply by asking: "How do you think I can help you?" Ordinarily, the response to this rather simple question will address both the client's problem and what the client thinks the advisor can do about it.

Since advising is a collaborative process and not all advisors are expert advice givers, it makes sense to ensure that you supply all of these items: Where you've been, where you are now, where you want to go, and how the advisor can help. We should cooperate with our advisors to make the process a success. It's best to think through these items in advance, and especially prepare ready answers to the question, "How do you think I can help you?" where "help" need not be limited to solutions or specific actions but could just consist of helping you think through your problem, seeing aspects that you're not seeing, helping you to figure out what your problem is, or if you even have a problem! The various forms of help are discussed in Chapter 2, "What Advice Does for You."

The following is a simple generic recipe for many advice-seeking situations where you have identified the prospective advisor:

1. Prepare for the contact with your advisor by learning his or her background and recent activities, consulting the Web, LinkedIn, Facebook, your notes on past exchanges, or people you know in common.

2. Anticipate questions that the advisor will ask himself or herself about you and your meeting with him or her, perhaps subconsciously. For example:
   a. Who is this person? (Such a question may occur to the advisor if he or she doesn't know you, or know much about you.)
   b. Is this worth my time?
   c. What does this person want?
   d. Am I the right person for this?
   e. Will I enjoy meeting this person?
   f. Am I just one of many targets, or am I special?

3. Contact the advisor, keeping in mind the previous questions (those in 2a-2f, above). For example, an email could consist of four brief paragraphs that contain:

   a. Something about the advisor's background or activities that shows you've prepared for the meeting.

   b. A reminder of who you are, how your paths have crossed before (if they have), people you know in common, and so on. This shows both humility and consideration on your part.

   c. Your situation and what you're looking for from the advisor—absent a very specific need, a fallback is to explain that you face some choice points and would appreciate the chance to "pick your brain on the subject."

   d. Your suggestion for follow-up: coffee, lunch phone, or some other meeting at a time and place that's convenient to the advisor. Face-to-face, if possible, is much, much better than over the phone.

4. Arrive early for a face-to-face meeting, before the advisor arrives. If meeting at a restaurant or coffee house, I prefer to wait at the restaurant entrance or on the sidewalk rather than inside at a table. Waiting before taking a table shows more courteous deference.

5. Make brief small talk, asking or commenting on—with genuine interest—the advisor's recent activities.

6. Explain your situation as best you can. Borrow from Salacuse's formula:

   a. Where have I been?

   b. Where am I now?

   c. Where do I want to go?

7. Ask for their thoughts. A generic fallback is to simply ask, "What do you think?" or "What advice would you give me?" More specific requests can come from revisiting the first three advice benefits from Chapter 2, "What Advice Does for You:"

   a. Solutions

      i. What would you do in my situation?

      ii. What would be bad choices?

      iii. What could go wrong if I follow a certain path?

     iv. Did you ever encounter a similar situation? How did it turn out? Is there anything you feel you should have done differently?

  b. Pointers (e.g., Who else could I talk to about this? Should I mention you?)

  c. Formulation

     i. What factors should I consider?

     ii. Am I missing anything in thinking about the issue?

8. Take notes. Bring a pen and paper.

9. If you have heard conflicting advice, bring it up and ask for their opinion.

10. Pay for lunch or coffee, as discreetly as possible. If your advisor objects, suggest that it's your privilege to show a tiny bit of gratitude. If your advisor objects twice, then yield, especially if he or she is much older or more senior than you. Possibly ask if the advisor has any final advice for you.

11. Later, if you make use of the advisor's recommendations, or if you saw the situation from a new angle due to your discussion, contact him or her to say so and express your appreciation for his or her time and energy. If the advisor is a busy person, then just send email or leave voicemail.

12. If there is a short-term outcome, then skip step #11 but combine it with information on the outcome of your process, whichever way it went, and explain how the advisor influenced what you did. In other words, *close the loop* with advisors by letting them know the outcome and relating that outcome to the help they provided.

In view of the *forbidden fruit* or *reactance* phenomenon (see Chapter 5, "What Research Says") of actively rejecting advice that contradicts one's formed preferences, it's better to avoid making preliminary choices before gathering advice. While preparing to get advice, try to keep an open mind and focus on identifying the possible courses of action and their pros and cons, while realizing that you may miss an option, a pro, or a con. Don't try to pick a frontrunner beforehand. Keeping an open mind does require tolerating uncertainty over a period of time without getting too anxious.

Never perform a bait-and-switch, where you pretend to seek advice from someone but actually have a different goal. For example, never ask someone for career advice when your true goal is to seek a job from that person.

In summary, structuring an advice session should be done with forethought. Observe simple and even refined courtesies. Recall that helpful advice doesn't just consist of solutions but also pointers, new ways to frame the problem, validation and moral support, legitimation, and even human engagement and empathy. Remember that an initial outreach can be a solid foundation for the future, and you never get a second chance to make a first impression.

At the start of this chapter, Whitehead called for civilization to advance by being able to perform more operations without thinking. Advice seekers still have to think, because their own circumstances are unique and so are their advisor's. However, structuring advice sessions is not so unique, so this chapter proposes a recipe you can use so that your creative thinking can focus on your problem's details and on weighing the advice received.

Our map of the terrain is almost complete. We can now recognize situations that call out for advice and identify, approach, and meet with good advisors. The final map fragment, without which many travelers will lose their way, even while they are able to clearly see the goal, needs attention. The next chapter will deal with the likelihood of receiving contradictory advice.

Chapter 11: Dealing with Contradictory Advice

Earlier I told the story of how, while planning to raise external capital to help grow our software company (Vivisimo) faster, I sought advice on how best to do it, getting three contradictory recommendations from three accomplished former CEOs:

- Raise the capital myself.

- Hire a Chief Financial Officer (CFO) to lead the effort, but work closely together.

- Hire an agent to raise the capital who would be compensated by a percentage of the funds that were raised.

I was surprised but not shocked. After considering the options carefully, I opted to recruit a CFO. That worked well and we raised the capital.

High-level conflicting advice is not unusual, and in general, contradictions in life are common. I mentioned earlier that Herbert A. Simon, my academic advisor during my time as a graduate student, was fond of pointing out that truisms of folk wisdom come in seemingly contradictory pairs. His point was that folk wisdom, even if true, depended greatly on the circumstances, which were up to you to understand.

At the opposite extreme, *scientific* knowledge is believed by most non-scientists to be based on consensus among scientists. Sometimes consensus is breached publicly when scientific disagreements become public controversies, as with the issue of global warming/climate change, but these public disputes are often attributed to dishonesty, excess ambition, personal rivalries, or other vices. What non-scientists don't realize is that at the forefront of science, where all *research* scientists work, there is disagreement among research scientists *themselves* about the most important matters! These disagreements usually aren't because one group disbelieves another's facts but because scientists disagree on what's important, what theories best explain the facts, what facts need to be accounted for, whether a theory really does explain the observations, and so on.

My point is that nobody should be surprised, much less dismayed, by receiving contradictory advice, since informal folk wisdom at one extreme, and leading-edge science at the other extreme, are filled with conflicting ideas. In short: *Even experts disagree.* The necessary task is to deal with contradictions—don't get unnerved but instead understand the reasons behind the conflicting advice, take the best ideas, and forge an informed course of action.

To check if it's generally appreciated that folk and expert knowledge are filled with contradictions, I did a Web search on *dealing with contradictory advice*, which turned up as the top result a philosophy forum (see http://wsupf.wikidot.com/forum/t-144424) at Wayne State University. I'll quote from two Web postings on that site:

> Slow and steady wins the race.
> A stitch in time saves nine.
> The early bird gets the worm.
>
> These seem on their face to be at least somewhat contradictory. If I want to succeed, it seems I should act quickly, given the second two pieces of advice. But I should also act slowly, given the first. What is a poor soul to do?
>
> The answer is that these are really dealing with different issues. The second two pieces of advice tell you when you ought to act, and the first tells you how you ought to perform the action. You should act immediately, as soon as possible. But you should not hurry—instead, you should perform the action slowly and steadily.

> Another way to make sense of this is to say that the second two really do urge quickness, and that the first is advice about the true nature of quickness. It says that the quickest way to accomplish your goal is to perform it slowly and steadily. So the second two say "act quickly", and the first tells you how to do that.
>
> Do you agree with this analysis? Furthermore, do you agree with the advice?

The post above got the following reply:

> Any "validity" of *any* advice presupposes the vanity of "freewill/choice." I do not entertain any such belief.
> We are what we are, every moment. Some appear wise, some less so, etc. We are who we are. No options available.
> I suggest that "advice" plays more to the ego of the adviser than to his "victim."

From these two Web posts, both of which I disagree with, I conclude that there is general confusion about the nature of contradiction.

How Contradiction Arises

Let's try to understand where contradictions can arise. Chapter 2 "What Advice Does for You," lists three such areas: (1) Solutions, (2) Pointers, and (3) Framing. Two advisors might (1) recommend different incompatible solutions; (2) differ on the value of consulting another individual, document, or information source; and (3) disagree on the importance of a certain dimension, such as the future resale value of a new house or automobile, or whether to consider the quality of local schools when young newlyweds are buying a first house.

I believe there are six major sources of contradiction from qualified advisors:

1. An advisor has *experience* with one course of action but not with others, either by accident or because of his own circumstances.

125

Raul Valdes-Perez

In my previous story about getting contradictory advice from three former CEOs about the best way to raise investment capital, I believe that all of them were basing their recommendations on what they had personally done in the past, successfully. Similarly, I often advocate a gap year as an exchange student abroad before starting college, because it worked wonders for me in my life.

2. Advisors have different *values*. For example, if the problem is a troubled marriage and the question is whether to divorce, one advisor might believe that marriage should be permanent and troubles should be worked out, whereas another advisor might see marriage as a partnership that can be dissolved if the union isn't agreeable. If the issue is whether and when to quit a job, one advisor may factor in loyalty while another doesn't.

3. An advisor may have issues related to his or her own *self-interest* in the outcome. This need not be negative: A parent's self-interest or aspirations for a child may lead the parent to recommend one career path, whereas a disinterested advisor would not.

4. An advisor's *mistaken perception of your circumstances or goals* can lead to advice that conflicts with other advice you've received. I recall a lunch with a prominent local business executive who gave me unsolicited advice that assumed—wrongly—that I had the goal of maximizing my personal financial benefit above other considerations. This possibility of misunderstanding another's needs and wants is another reason why it's important to have advisors who will listen and understand your situation, and another reason that you should *proactively* provide them with the details that they'll need in order to advise you well.

5. An advisor might understand your circumstances and goals but *misjudge* the chances that a course of action will succeed or fail. An optimist will judge the likelihoods differently than a pessimist. Maybe the advisor had a positive outcome, but only because his or her personal qualities were suited to the task. For example, an extrovert might recommend a course that an introvert would not be suited to follow.

6. Advisors may need to make *assumptions about future events* or trends, but disagree about the probabilities of these events and

126

trends. This happens a lot, since accurately predicting the future is a losing game. For example, career and entrepreneurship advice implicitly involves judgments of whether certain professions and markets will go boom or bust, and advisors' crystal balls will be cloudy, each in a distinct way.

Dealing with Contradiction

The following steps can help you to better understand or deal with the six sources of contradiction:

1. Try to understand the advisor's own previous choices. Besides his or her own recommendations, did he or she try other courses of action and find them unsatisfactory? Is the advisor's experience limited to one course of action? Asking for the advisor's opinion of the pros and cons of the alternatives should be telling. If advisors cannot articulate the pros and cons, then their experience may be narrow.

2. Ask yourself how the advisor might have a stake in your outcome beyond simply your health, wealth, and happiness.

3. Be sure to convey your circumstances and goals, whether or not you've been asked about them. If the advisor doesn't seem interested in those, then get a different advisor or ask generic questions like "What should I be aware of?" or "Whom else could I consult?"

4. Try to identify tacit assumptions that underlie the advisor's reasoning. For example, ask what needs to be true, or what has to happen, in order to have success with the suggested course of action. These assumptions should include external events and trends whose likelihood the advisor is implicitly relying on.

5. Politely point out other recommendations you've received, together with their assumptions and reasoning, and ask the advisor for his or her opinion about them. It's important not to imply that this advisor's advice is suspect. Just state that you are hearing conflicting advice, that you understand that it's the nature of things, that you are trying to puzzle your way through, and that you would appreciate thoughts on the multiple options you've been given by others.

At the end of this process you'll need to weigh what you've heard and decide how to proceed. You could enlist a partner to help you decide, probably a good friend or family member. Describe the decision situation and work through the recommendations and the best course of action with that other person.

Alternatively, following the famous advice of Benjamin Franklin in a 1772 letter to Joseph Priestley, the 18th century British scientist and theologian, you could over the course of a few days list the pros and cons of a course of action in two columns. Then you could delete offsetting pros and cons in each column. You may have two pros offsetting one con, or vice versa. At the end of the process, you should be left with a single pro or a single con that cannot be crossed out or offset, and that will determine your answer.

Chapter 5, "What Research Says," pointed out that people sometimes will discount *all* offered advice when it's contradictory. Common sense also tells us that people sometimes consult only one advisor because they anticipate the paralyzing effects of contradictory advice. So keep in mind that centuries-old folk wisdom at one extreme, scientific research at the other, and everywhere in between are full of contradiction, without malice playing any role at all. If you understand why contradictions happen, you'll be less likely to become unnerved.

We have completed our own map of the advice-seeking terrain, benefiting from our earlier surveying and from the scouting reports of predecessors. We should now be able to recognize situations that call out for advice, identify, approach, and meet with good advisors, and deal with their conflicting recommendations. While traversing the terrain, however, there are interesting stops along the way—boulders and watering holes, if you will—that deserve some descriptions of their own in our next chapters.

Chapter 12: The Role of the Web and Social Media

Suppose Roger is planning a two-week vacation. Instead of picking a destination that he's already visited or has heard of, he decides to turn to external sources for advice. It's late evening, so he searches the Web for vacation ideas and is overwhelmed by the number of choices, since every location has something to recommend it. By now it's 11 p.m., so he tries Twitter, since he has hundreds of followers on his Twitter account. He tweets, "Planning a 2-week vacation and looking for recommended destinations." He gets a flurry of replies from people he barely knows, including, "Try Sanibel island in Florida. Great shelling beaches, which kids love." and "Look at Santo Domingo in Dominican Republic. Lots of history and great merengue dancing."

However, Roger's two children are in college and have other plans, the vacation is for July, and he dreads heat and humidity, since he grew up in Montana and isn't used to it. Moreover, his wife Rosalind really likes nightlife, but they are looking for something more like dinner theater than dancing the night away. Also, neither Roger nor Rosalind feels comfortable visiting another country that doesn't speak English. Oh, and they live in Oregon, not in the East, so Florida and the Dominican Republic are long flights. And the children's college expenses are making it hard to spend much this year.

Roger realizes that his Twitter respondents knew little of this. He considers making another tweet or Facebook post that points out these circumstances but decides against doing so because he is uncomfortable sharing all this personal information with casual acquaintances. The people who know him well don't bother responding, since they were among the hundreds that Roger reached out to on Twitter and they figure that somebody else will respond, even though they'd gladly provide all the help Roger needed if he sought them out individually.

Roger's situation illustrates the relevance of important questions about the role of the Web and social media in relation to Roger's advice seeking goal: To confidently and convincingly explain—to himself and others—why a certain course of action is right for him and Rosalind and other actions are wrong, worse, or too uncertain. Here are some of the important questions:

- For what problems are the Web and social media *not good enough*?
- What problems are Web and social media good enough for?
- Do the best potential advisors respond to mass queries?
- How can the Web and social media improve in the future to more closely resemble personalized advice and the quality it produces?

Let's look at each of these questions now in the sections that follow.

For what Problems are the Web and Social Media *not Good Enough*?

Let's see which of the advice-seeking accounts in this book could have been handled by the Web or social media rather than by personalized advice.

The following accounts appear in the book:

1. Conrad's quest to study electronics engineering (Chapter 1)

2. Abraham Lincoln's deliberations on freeing the slaves (Chapter 2)

3. Daisy looking for a job after graduation (Chapter 2)

4. My application to engineering grad schools (Chapter 3)

5. My daughter looking for an internship after her freshman year at college (Chapter 3)

6. Planning an approach to looking for investment capital (Chapter 3)

7. Eddie's struggle to live within his means by rearranging his eating habits (Chapter 7)

8. My evaluation of a technology-based business idea (Chapter 8)

9. Elizabeth looking for a career change (Chapter 9)

10. My scouting of potential vice presidents of engineering (Chapter 10)

11. My setting up of a legal and financial instrument (Chapter 10)

12. Being consulted by Samantha on technical aspects of her start-up (Chapter 10)

13. Asking an Indiana park officer about beach locations (Chapter 2)

I believe that the Web and social media are good enough for *very few* of these 13 cases. The easiest is the one that starts off this book: A foreign student thinking mistakenly that only two U.S. colleges in the mid-1970s offered education in electronics engineering. Such questions about easily established facts—"Who teaches electronics engineering?"—are readily answered on the Web. But harder to answer are these: "Of the colleges that teach electronics engineering, which should I apply to, and which should I attend if admitted? Should I pick a college based on a major? Should I even commit to a major before starting college?"

Most of these stories are not amenable to Web-only advice for the usual reason: The right course of action depends strongly on one's circumstances and goals, which cannot easily be factored in to the advice one finds on the Web.

We can find support for this view within Media Richness Theory, which is a framework for describing a communications medium, such as face-to-face, video conferencing, telephone, email, posters, and so on. The theory, originated by R. A. Daft and R. H. Lengel, links "… media richness to social presence. It has been argued that FTF [face-to-face] differs significantly than other environments because it exudes a greater perception of presence than other media. Media that are not sufficiently rich have … a lower social presence than media that are high in richness. […] a rich media is one that exudes a greater social presence and a higher social presence implies a richer communicative media" (in *Encyclopedia of Information Ethics and Security* by M.

Quigley). Seeking advice on highly individualized issues, often fraught with emotion, certainly benefits from a social presence.

What Problems Are the Web and Social Media *Good Enough* For?

In general, I'd say that the Web and social media are good enough, by themselves, on: (1) factual problems whose solutions we don't normally consider to be *advice*; (2) issues where wrong decisions don't matter much, for example, Netflix recommending a movie or Amazon recommending a book; and (3) problems that have yielded successfully to someone's careful case-by-case analysis, resulting in an open procedure that someone else can follow that leads to recommended solutions. These procedures are sometimes called decision trees because the later questions depend on the replies to the earlier ones. Let's simply call them decision rules and look at some examples.

1. **Should I seek advice?** Chapter 7, "When You Should Seek Advice," lists more than 20 questions that you can answer—at AdviceIsForWinners.com under Tools or on paper—and get a score and recommendation of whether to seek advice on a specific problem.

2. **What *Last Will and Testament* are right for me?** Legal websites, such as RocketLawyer.com, will ask you many questions about wishes and circumstances before generating a fully formed legal document such as a last will.

3. **Should I itemize my deductions?** Tax-return preparation websites such as TurboTax will help you make many decisions—not just whether to itemize—based on your situation and presumed goal to save on taxes.

4. **What percent of a start-up company should each co-founder own?** An entrepreneur, investor, and blogger named Dan Shapiro wrote a decision rule that calculates an ownership split among a start-up's co-founders based on seniority, who contributed the idea, who worked on the prototype, who's the CEO, who's full-time, who put in cash, and so on: geekwire.com/2011/wrong-answer-5050-calculating-cofounder-equity-split

Frank Demmler at Carnegie Mellon University published on the Web an alternative approach, which he called the Founders' Pie Calculator.

In each of the four cases, knowledgeable people thought hard about the varying circumstances and how they match up with actions. The resulting decision rules might be the basis for a paid service or just a published contribution to the world's knowledge. If you can find rules that anticipate and accommodate your situation, then they are a good approximation to getting skilled, personalized advice, as long as the decision rules are well crafted.

However, crafting general rules is difficult. For example, Shapiro answered a commenter on the cited website:

> It's very true this is only rules of thumb. My first version of the article was filled with so many caveats and exceptions that it was unreadable. So I decided to rip them all out and count on the fact that nobody thinks I'm smart enough to be right all the time.

Shapiro confesses that he found the task too complex and decided to simplify it by ignoring exceptional circumstances, which might well match yours. Moreover, Shapiro's article clearly explains that other experts disagree with his approach. So writing such decision rules is hard, different experts can disagree, and the rules might even need to change over time as laws change or new knowledge becomes relevant. (All these provisos apply as well to my own rules for deciding when to seek advice.) Nevertheless, Shapiro's and Demmler's rules provide advice based on experts (themselves), which may well be superior to what's available within one's potential circle of advisors.

The issue of finding Web sources that are superior to one's own potential circle brings up the credibility question: Who is knowledgeable and unbiased, in the sense of not having an ulterior motive of trying to sell you something? General principles can apply, whether evaluating advisors that you seek out or writers on the Web. For example, an advisor or writer should be able to fairly discuss the pros and cons of competing alternatives, even ones that conflict with his or her own recommendations. In addition, it's a good sign if a Web posting is followed by intelligent commentary by readers who can point out arguments that the author missed, as in the case of Shapiro's cited article on the website.

"Recommender systems" such as those at Amazon.com that point out items that other shoppers bought together with the displayed item, or at Netflix that recommend a film based on your previous rentals, provide advice of a sort. However, these systems recommend easily inspectable alternatives rather than intangible courses of action. The problem with recommender systems is that they don't explain their recommendations in human terms, that is, in terms that answer the question, "Why should I see this movie?" Recommenders who can't help advice seekers to explain a decision to themselves and others don't inspire trust and confidence. Unless the issue is trivial, that's a big drawback.

In our comparison of the merits of personal advisors versus Web and social media, we've focused on the *type* of problem that is calling for advice. But characteristics of advice seekers *themselves* can influence the relative value of the Web and social media. For example, if the advice seeker's social capital is poor, then the Web and social media may be the only good options. One could say that a great contribution of the Web is to make the socially handicapped and the shy better able to leverage the knowledge of others through Internet-mediated dialogue.

Do the Best Potential Advisors Respond to Mass Queries?

Scholarly research has shown that recipients of mass email messages are less likely to respond if they are just one of a crowd ("Electronic Helping Behavior: The Virtual Presence of Others Makes a Difference," in the journal *Basic and Applied Social Psychology*, 2005). On simple factual questions, it doesn't matter, since the inquirer needs only one correct reply, or several replies if verifying correctness isn't straightforward. So even if the likelihood of an individual reply goes down, increasing the number of recipients can lead to a better result.

However, on problems involving judgment, the quality of replies matters greatly. On my interpretation, these research results suggest that social media will suffer from the same problem: Any given individual, for example, those who would offer the best advice, is less likely to take the trouble to respond, much less to understand one's circumstances and goals, when approached as part of a social mass.

How Can the Web and Social Media Improve in the Future to Narrow the Gap in Quality Between It and Personalized Advice?

Clayton Christensen, a Harvard Business School professor, argues brilliantly in his books that complicated and/or costly products and services are sometimes undercut by innovations that incumbents at first disdain as inferior. However, these innovations expand the market by (1) reaching nonconsumers who are put off by the cost or complexity of the current choices, and by (2) improving over time so that the quality gap narrows. For example, discount retailers have disrupted full-service department stores, and mobile phones have disrupted landline telephones. In the future, online education may disrupt traditional on-campus higher education, and routine legal services may be disrupted by online offerings that provide standard templates.

Are the same forces at play in advice seeking? That is, will the advisory process, in essence a collaborative, highly personal exchange of the advice seeker's circumstances and goals and the advisor's knowledge and wisdom, be undercut by simpler interactions based on the Web and social media? One way this could happen is if people come to perceive—wrongly in my view—that Web and social media interactions are good enough for the purpose.

Another valuable lesson taught by my graduate school advisor is that human beings are poor at predicting the future. I don't know if the Web and social media will supplant highly personal advisory relationships, but for those media to have a chance, they must somehow elicit more of the advice seeker's circumstances and goals. Either expert software must be developed to take account of the variety of situations, or good human advisors must be motivated to participate in online advice giving. Issues of user privacy will need to be overcome.

Recommendations.

The Web is a fount of facts, opinions, and advice that makes numerous things easy that were hard or impractical before. The Web and social media should complement any advice seeker's more personalized outreach. Some obvious roles for these media, already discussed in other chapters, are to (1) *identify* potential advisors (for example, using LinkedIn, or by searching the Web for your topic AND your locale), and (2) *research the backgrounds and activities* of people you are going to meet with in order to show that you've taken the trouble to prepare for the meeting.

The other type of complementary work involves researching your *problem*, not researching potential advisors. Building on Chapter 2, "What Advice Does for You," the following are sub-tasks that the Web and social media are ideal for:

1. Try to find the range of possible solutions—including "do nothing"—to your problem. Combine your Web-search query with other phrases to try to identify the possibilities. For example, if

you've written a book and are considering self-publishing along with other, more traditional publishing options, try these queries:

  a. "self-publishing" AND "second approach"
  b. "self-publishing" AND "third approach"
  c. "self-publishing" AND "fourth approach"

2. Try to collect reasons to definitely avoid a solution or approach. For example, try searching for "avoid self publishing" or "avoiding self publishing" (Web search engines may give different results on these two search queries) and see what people say.

3. Look for review articles on the subject using queries like:

  a. "self-publishing" AND "review article"
  b. "self-publishing 101"
  c. "self-publishing" AND beginner
  d. "how to self-publish"
  e. "self-publishing for dummies"
  f. "advice for self-publishing" (or self-publishers)

4. Look for unconventional opinions that may point out dimensions or aspects of the problem that others miss. Try queries like:

  a. "self-publishing" AND skeptic (or skeptical, skepticism)
  b. "self-publishing" AND contrarian

Summarizing, in almost every case of advice seeking, the Web and social media are indispensable helpers for researching both your problem and your advisors. Recall what should be your goal: *To confidently and convincingly explain—to yourself and others—why a certain course of action is right for you and other actions are wrong, worse, or too uncertain.*

If the Web or social media can enable confident, convincing explanations, and you don't need personalized legitimation or ongoing support from advisors, and if you don't see this as an opportunity for constructive social engagement, or you are socially handicapped, then the Web and social media may be good enough for your needs and no personalized advice is needed. But for most problems that matter, complementing personalized advice seeking with Web work is the best course.

This chapter has looked at a very interesting and timely stop along our journey, which has elements both of a boulder and a watering hole. The Web boulder can flatten you if you rely on it exclusively. At the same time, the Web watering hole offers up refreshment that has no parallel and never suffers from a dry season. Next, we'll take up how to make advice seeking—drawing on the knowledge and wisdom of others through personal encounters—a regular part of one's life.

Chapter 13: Advice as a Rule, not an Exception

As mentioned early in this book, once I was driving along the 500 miles westward from Pittsburgh, my residence for the last 25 years, to my hometown of Chicago. I was nearing the entry into Illinois during rush hour from northern Indiana, along the shore of Lake Michigan. Having planned to avoid the rush-hour traffic, I had prepared a dinner that I planned to eat along some beach that I'd seek out, since I wasn't familiar with the area. After asking for directions, I arrived at the Indiana Dunes State Park along the lakefront. Rather than just pay the entrance fee and head for the beach, I opted to seek advice from the guard, as follows:

> Hello, Officer. I'm driving from Pittsburgh to Chicago, but thought to stop to visit and get a look at your Indiana beaches and have my dinner, which I brought with me in the car. What do you suggest?

The friendly guard explained that Indiana residents would pay $5 to enter but that an out-of-stater like me was charged $10. Instead, he added, I could go to the beach that the locals frequented, which was just a couple of minutes away. So that's what I did. I ate my prepared dinner, enjoyed the views, felt the sand (no sand in Pittsburgh!), and resumed my trip an hour later. The human interaction with the guard gave me a good feeling, I saved $10, and I had the pleasure of "going native" with the locals. I suspect that the guard was also left with the satisfaction of helping out a visitor by sharing his local knowledge. Only the state coffers were out $10.

The point of this little story is that by making such outreaches routine, where we automatically consider drawing on others' expertise just like we automatically consider eating when it's time or we're hungry, we can achieve these little satisfactions of a task well done, even for matters that aren't of great importance.

Advice seeking is not the only activity that should be made routine. *Closing the loop with advisors* should be made routine, if at all practical. The basic principle is that after finishing a task, whether picking a beach spot or a job or a college to attend, one should re-contact whoever gave advice or acted as a sounding board to inform them of the outcome—whether their advice was followed or not. The reasons include basic courtesy, satisfying the curiosity of the advice giver, and creating goodwill as a basis for future interactions with the advisor—even allowing for a role reversal where *they* draw on one's own expertise. Although an earlier chapter disparaged Ralph Waldo Emerson's essay on self-reliance, I'll quote with approval something else he wrote: "Good manners are made up of petty sacrifices."

Many times I've given advice and then never learned the outcome. Was the advice followed? If not, why not? What happened? If my advice wasn't followed, was there something I missed in the situation? If so, what was it? Maybe I can learn something as well. Being left hanging is especially unsatisfactory when the advice includes making an introduction to a third person, because any introduction puts at risk the introducer's reputation if the encounter did not go well, or if the advice seeker was rude.

Electronic communication makes closing the loop simple and unobtrusive: Just send a brief email with the outcome of your process, which can be read in seconds at the recipient's convenience. Even small issues are worth closing the loop on. For example, once I asked a business associate about sites to visit in Maine, his home state, which I would be visiting during a one-week vacation in New England. He recommended Kennebunkport as a destination, which I had not considered. After the vacation was over, I took the time to send this email:

> I just wanted to let you know that on vacation last week we visited Ogunquit beach (nice) and Kennebunkport (also), where we took a 2-hour sailing trip on a ketch and also had an excellent lobster dinner at Nunan's, a simple, relatively inexpensive place recommended by the captain's mate. Our

> base for these trips was Dover, NH. The water was cold but bearable for a Chicagoan who grew up in Lake Michigan's waters. My wife and daughter also emerged unscathed. Thanks for the Kennebunkport tip.

That message met with this gracious reply:

> Thank you for the update, I was thinking about you last week. I am glad to hear the trip went off well, and you all survived, and perhaps even enjoyed, Maine! I hope the rest of your travels were enjoyable as well.

Of course, sometimes it's impractical or obtrusive to circle back. For example, in my trip to the Indiana shoreline, I did not revisit the state park guard to let him know the outcome of my dinner hour on the Indiana beach before continuing on my way.

It has taken me many years to perfect the practice of closing the loop with advice givers. I just wish I had thought of this long before I did finally become aware of it, since I missed many opportunities to create goodwill and satisfy my advisors' curiosity about what happened.

On April 25, 2012, IBM announced publicly its intent to acquire Vivisimo, nearly twelve years after its founding. Anticipating the announcement, I spent a few hours compiling a list of several dozen people who had helped our efforts throughout those years, or even encouraged us to found the company, and phoned or sent them news of the announcement that same day, with my thanks. Besides being the right thing to do, it spread goodwill and was appreciated.

People don't ponder every day whether they should eat, sleep, get up, visit the bathroom, say hello, open a door for someone, walk through a door being opened for them, go to bed, and so on. Advice seeking can join in this routine, not because it's done always and every day, but because it always come to mind naturally as an option, as a matter of course.

This chapter has paused along our journey at another watering hole that has the potential for lifelong refreshment if just treated with a little care. Our next stop will seek inspiration from a big watering hole—an oasis—one that supports a community that intensely practices advice seeking.

Chapter 14: A Peek at an Advice-Centric Environment

If we can identify and study a culture that thrives on advice seeking and advice giving, we can draw inspiration for how it could work in our everyday personal and work lives. We don't have to go to remote or exotic locales, since suitable ones are close to home: elite graduate schools of science, which have been phenomenally successful at directly creating new knowledge and new technologies, and educating new cadres of people to do the same elsewhere. Let's examine how they are set up, drawing on this author's personal experience at three institutions: MIT's computer science research labs in the middle 1980s, Carnegie Mellon University's computer science department from 1986 through 2001, and earlier the University of Illinois at Chicago, a large state school. I'll mostly draw on my longest experience at Carnegie Mellon in Pittsburgh, Pennsylvania.

Acculturation

Let's accompany "Jane" in her graduate school career, say, at Carnegie Mellon's graduate program in computer science. When Jane arrives, she spends the first month getting acclimated and learning to better understand how the system works and what is expected of her. Her key graduation goal is to carry out successful research by making a solid contribution to knowledge in the field, which means she should identify a significant question about computers that is not yet answered, that would have practical impact on the field if it were answered, and that others would care about. All of this is new to her, since as an undergraduate Jane mostly learned textbook material and showed her mastery of course content by solving homework and test problems, and maybe writing essays that expand on something she learned in her books. Research is a whole new game requiring a completely different set of skills. Many people before her have gone through what Jane will face, including all of the professors in Jane's department, who were once fresh-faced graduate students themselves. Elite graduate schools are set up to facilitate this transfer of knowledge, experience, and feedback from experts and more senior peers to novices.

At Carnegie Mellon, the first month was devoted to a so-called Immigration Course, whose goals were to create peer solidarity, acquaint students with the work going on in the department, with what they would need to accomplish in order to graduate, and with tips on this unfamiliar beast called research, in those days delivered by Herbert A. Simon, a giant of the department. As previously stated, Simon was a Nobel Laureate in Economics as well as one of the founders of the Carnegie Mellon Computer Science Department when such departments were still a novelty because computers themselves were recent novelties.

In his annual "What is Research?" lecture, Simon would pose questions that students should often ask themselves over the coming years as they tried to formulate a topic for their graduate research. Among the key questions were:

1. If you are tackling a problem that others have worked on, what is your "secret weapon" that will let you succeed where others haven't? An unacceptable answer is "I'm smarter than those others," since it's rarely true. Better answers are "I have access to instruments that others lacked," or "Recent progress in peripheral areas newly enables solving the problem now, unlike before."

2. A research problem is a question, not a topic. Experience has shown that students can fail to make progress because they spend their time thinking about general areas rather than trying to narrow things down to something with a question mark at the end that begs for an answer. Thus, they work on something like "collaborative document-writing over the Internet" rather than a specific question like "How does collaboratively writing a document differ when 10+ people across the planet are working together, rather than two people in the same time zone, and what

capabilities are needed to support these differences?" So what question are you trying to answer?

3. Would anybody care whether you solved the problem? Fundamental research is often self-driven, rather than driven by a boss with a problem to solve or by industry with a pressing need. If it's the latter, it's called applied research. Self-driven research, usually called curiosity-driven, can lead to work on trivialities that nobody cares about, like determining how the number of spots on a butterfly varies with the average regional temperature.

Formal Advisors

Armed with such insights from her predecessors in this long tradition, Jane ends her one-month orientation course and is expected to begin research work while she takes required graduate-level coursework. However, she is not left to sink or swim but is assigned, or chooses, an advisor who normally will stay with Jane during her entire graduate-student career, which can last four to six years at most institutions. The advisor's job is not to help Jane with her personal life, or even so much with her career, but to turn her into a competent researcher, ideally combining that goal with his own goal of leading a high-quality research program and attracting the funding to sustain it and pay the way of grad students.

In my own first year as a graduate student at Carnegie Mellon, I had two advisors, which was unusual but not rare. I asked to be assigned two advisors (John McDermott and Herbert Simon) because I figured that if I could learn a lot from one advisor, then from two I could learn twice as much, or maybe 1 1/2 times as much. I also joked with my classmates and friends that I would have a weekly meeting with one advisor, who might ask me a question to ponder, which I then posed to the second for his insights, which I would then regurgitate to the first (of course, I was joking!—I never did this). McDermott left Carnegie Mellon after my first year, so I remained with Simon as my sole formal advisor until graduating five years later. The photo of us on the next page was taken in Simon's home.

The advisor/student relationship varies from one department to another, and according to the working styles of the professor or even of the student. For example, in Biology there is an emphasis on groups, since students will work on their experiments in the same lab with shared instruments and materials and so need ready access to guidance from more senior students. In other cases, for example, in computer science, a student could work on his own and didn't need the whole structure and support of a lab group. In my case at Carnegie Mellon, Prof. Simon met with all his student advisees one-on-one for the standard weekly or biweekly one-hour appointment.

What goes on at such advisor meetings? In my case, there were two recurring activities: (1) asking Simon his opinion on a particular question, and (2) describing my work in progress and asking him for feedback or suggestions of any sort. My reasons for (1) were that Simon knew a lot about many things, even outside of science, and had unique perspectives that were certainly different from mine. So in the course of my reading and work during the previous week, I would write down the questions that I wanted to ask him. I can mention several that Simon answered in his characteristically clear-headed and simple style, which taught me a lot. Once I asked him if he thought the university tenure system was unfair, in the sense that a bright young assistant professor would toil for six years or more and then possibly be denied tenure (a permanent job, revocable only for reasons of ethics or delinquency), which in effect is a slow-motion firing. Simon explained that the tenure system was intended to uphold high standards—which I knew—and that when professors were denied tenure, they didn't "go on the bread lines;" they went elsewhere to develop their careers. It was a very simple observation, but one which I, as a young graduate student, would not have thought of myself. It placed things permanently in a new perspective.

My favorite example from these years of one-on-one meetings is a question whose answer helped me to make general sense of, to mentally categorize, a broad range of work in science. Simon's seed idea, which he developed through his career and for which he was recognized with a 1978 Nobel Prize, is that decision making in organizations is based on what Simon called "satisficing" rather than optimizing. The idea behind "satisficing" is that people make complex decisions by exploring a few options, gathering some limited information, and then choosing a satisfactory course of action

146

among several courses of action. This sounds extremely obvious, but classical economists disagreed: They conceive of humans as hyper-rationalists who optimize the expected satisfaction or "utility" by maximizing over all the possible courses of action, taking account of all available information, or at least closely approximating this behavior. My question for Simon was this: Can't you view the "satisficers"—those people who use limited means with limited information to pick a satisfactory course of action from a limited set—as "optimizers" who are minimizing their toil, or balancing those exertions against the work needed to find something satisfactory? In other words, can't the whole process be brought under the optimizing mindset, by enlarging the criteria that people are using, to include the duration and costs of their exertion?

Simon's reply put much of science in perspective: You can always conceptualize something within a given framework. The important question is what will be gained by doing so. Specifically, if you conceive of a problem in one framework rather than another, then the chosen framework will inevitably lead you down a certain path that may not be fruitful if the framework isn't a good match. To illustrate, let's consider the police work of investigating a death. If the police frame the death as a homicide, then a homicide detective will be called in and will pose standard questions: Who was the last to see the victim alive? Who had something to gain from the victim's death? If the cause of death was a weapon, where is it? If instead the death is framed as a natural occurrence, then other paths are followed. Finally, if the death is suspected to be a case of alien body (or soul) snatching, then perhaps NASA or the CIA will be called, at least in TV land. Does experience teach us that calling NASA or calling a homicide detective is the better step? If calling the detective is better, then framing the death as a regular *murder* with a *victim* and a (human) *perpetrator* is the better framework. So the framework is destiny, in a way. Simon's advice—to pick the right framework to make sense of an issue by seeing where the framework will invariably lead—was priceless.

Besides the fanciful case of the TV homicide detective, a couple of other cases come to mind where the framework is destiny. I recall a high school graduation ceremony that I attended. The commencement speaker was an alumna of that school and her subsequent career led her to some fame as an author. The climax of her speech, when a commencement speaker offers pearls of advice to the eager graduates, had the speaker advising the high-school audience that whenever in the future they enter a room or a new situation, they should ask themselves: "Who's being oppressed here?" I just about fell out of my chair when I heard this. So the framework that this speaker was encouraging was that of oppressor/oppressed: Who is oppressing whom? How to help the oppressed to overcome or counteract the oppressor? How to reform or remove the oppressor? How is *that* for a default frame of reference to take into life as an 18-year-old emerging into the larger world?

Another example comes from a talk that Carnegie Mellon's Career and Professional Development Services invited me to give to graduating students, offering tips on job-seeking and general career advice. On the latter subject, I told the audience about a chapter from the book *Winning* by Jack Welch, the former CEO of General Electric, that we at Vivisimo handed out to every new employee hired. The chapter, "Sorry, No Shortcuts," advises youth who are starting at a first or a new job. Its wisdom boils down to two points: *Do more than is expected of you*, and *Don't be a pain in the neck*. After I gave examples of what it means to do more than is expected, a skeptical student asked how to avoid being exploited, because everyone would raise their expectations of you and expect you to do grunt work that others aren't willing to do. I was surprised by the question and didn't handle it well, replying only that being vigilant about exploitation was not the best mindset, that having others rely on you is a good problem to have, that you are not a slave, and that you'll always have the recourse of seeking another job if the situation is poor. Upon later reflection, I recalled that my first job during high school was as a restaurant dishwasher. On my first day, I was given an especially grimy cooking pan to clean, and I left that pan cleaner than it must have been in a very long time. After that, the cook always wanted *me* to clean that pan and to leave it spotless each time, which I was happy to oblige a few more times. Notwithstanding this story, I believe that Welch's framework—"What can I do here to surpass expectations?"—will lead to much better results for newcomers to the workforce than "Am I being exploited?"

Progressing Through the Program

Returning to Jane: After she has completed the orientation and has selected or been assigned an advisor, she takes graduate-level courses, does background reading in research areas that interest her, and maybe begins some small hands-on work on her own or as part of her advisor's ongoing projects, while meeting regularly with her advisor. When Jane makes enough progress that she has ideas or results to share with others, she may arrange to give a presentation to her peers, or anyone else who wishes to attend, as an open-attendance student seminar. Generally, the style in these seminars is polite but pointed: If the ideas are faulty or disregard other work that directly impacts their value, practicality, or originality, then Jane will hear it from her audience. Jane is expected to have a thick skin and not to take criticism or tough questioning personally, since this is part of the culture.

As Jane progresses, she may generate new research ideas that she will submit for publication in a scholarly conference or even a print journal. Her submitted article will be reviewed by experts, typically other academics, who let loose with their reactions and feel little constraint to be polite, since the encounters are not face-to-face and are even anonymous, so that the usual conventions of public politeness are not observed. In my own career, I recall one especially brutal reviewer who wrote that he couldn't fathom why the author felt that this line of research could possibly lead to anything worthwhile! Although hard to swallow, these reactions must be taken in stride as part of the process of advising and hardening young researchers to accept (severe) criticism and temporary defeat, to become their own competent self-critics, and to learn to critique others' work. In my experience, even distinguished senior scientists receive severe negative feedback on some of their work. The best reaction is to build on the criticism, at least by coming to an understanding of how best to present the ideas. This is the culture of science, and no shame is attached to giving or receiving such reactions or "advice."

If Jane is studying and working in an experimental science like most areas of biology, chemistry, physics, and many areas of computer science and social science, she will have another rich source of "advisory" feedback: nature itself. Much of science involves knowledge of the form "If I do this, then that will happen."

Even observational sciences like zoology, which observe, say, that black widows and praying mantises eat their mates, are saying that "If you observe a black widow or praying mantis after mating, it will (often) eat its mate." Likewise in computer science, if you design an interface following specific principles, then users (who are also part of nature) will make fewer mistakes. So nature chimes in with constant advisory clues to students about what works and what doesn't. Nature won't have a dialogue with you about your professional goals and circumstances, and won't provide explanations of why something didn't work, but at least it's never wrong, since it's the gold standard for science, because science studies nature.

After a few years of this, Jane will be ready for a public presentation of her dissertation or thesis. Jane's thesis committee, chaired by her advisor and rounded out with other professors or external experts, will read and criticize drafts of her thesis document and prepare Jane for her public thesis defense which, as the name suggests, involves public scrutiny of her results, which can be criticized by anyone who cares to attend, since thesis defenses are open forums. If the defense goes well, Jane is done, except for revisions to the thesis document that the thesis committee requests based on its members' or the public's questioning.

In summary, elite graduate schools in science are set up to provide continual advice to graduate students as they learn to become researchers. By convention, students are expected to seek advice from their professors and their peers, as well as the canned "advice" (knowledge) that is available from books and articles. In turn, students are expected to freely offer advice to peers and even faculty. No student ever has reason to feel embarrassed to seek advice, since the norms reinforce the advice giving process at every turn, from the first day until the last. Defensiveness in answering questions, or even in hearing criticism, is perceived as a weakness and a sign of immaturity and lack of confidence. Research graduate schools are one of those pockets of life where *not* seeking advice is unusual, even self-defeating, behavior. Of course there are others, such as health care, where few people feel inadequate or shy about seeking qualified health advice from medical professionals.

I cannot generalize too much, however, since my direct experience is limited. For example, as a graduate student I took a graduate-level seminar in psychology that had about ten students and was led by a professor. I was struck by the seeming emphasis on feelings as opposed to hard truth. I say this because the default behavior when one student wanted to disagree with another was to start off with a preamble about how the previous opinion was insightful, carefully considered, articulately expressed, a legitimate viewpoint, or whatever, followed by (indirectly) pointing out why the previous opinion was wrong. I confess that I preferred a less roundabout style, which serves to thicken the skin and prepare one for even highly critical advice.

Nothing's Perfect

However, advice seeking in graduate schools of research is pretty much limited to advice about research itself. There are other questions, however, that a student might want to seek advice on that are outside the normal scope of what goes on. For example:

- What factors should I consider in picking an advisor?
- How should I pick an area of specialization? Are there reliable trends that signal areas that will be growing or areas that are in decline?

- Is a career as a research scientist right for me?

- Do I want to emulate my graduate school advisor by pursuing an academic career? In sciences like biology, this means doing a "postdoc"—a two-to-three-year, low-paid job as a junior researcher attached to a senior professor's laboratory. What are the pros and cons of this career path?

Even in a culture dedicated to advising young graduate students, as reflected in the formal title of *advisor*, there are many questions for which advice seeking is not supported in the normal course of affairs. In such cases, Jane is no different from "Clarence," who took a job after his college graduation, except that Jane is surrounded by many peers in her same boat who *could* act as a sounding board, and that Jane has a formal advisor who *might* agree to offer advice outside of the conventional, expected area of *research advice*. This aspect of graduate-student life is captured hilariously in several "Piled Higher and Deeper" cartoons by Jorge Cham (www.phdcomics.com), who did a Ph.D. in mechanical engineering at Stanford and later was an instructor and researcher at Caltech. You can find these cartoons by visiting http://adviceisforwinners.com/grad-school-advice.

An interesting question is what happens to Jane after she graduates. My observations suggest that Jane will revert to the usual pattern, where advice seeking is rarer than in her graduate school due to all the reasons discussed in Chapter 3, "28 Reasons for Not Seeking Advice." The culture of expectations and norms determines the behaviors. But there is no reason why Jane cannot bring her graduate school principles and practices into her life and work, applying them beyond just research.

This chapter has described in detail an advice-intensive oasis that can serve as an inspiration even if the oasis may be fenced off to us in our own travels. There is one more landmark to be described in our next chapter: How advice seeking can vary across national cultures

Chapter 15: Advice Seeking in Different Cultures

In their 2011 article in the *Journal of Cross-Cultural Psychology* ("Let Me Tell You What to Do: Cultural Differences in Advice-Giving"), Y. E. Chentsova-Dutton and A. Vaughn reported on the habits and attitudes toward advice giving among Russians in Russia, Russian immigrants to the United States, and European Americans. Starting with anecdotal evidence that Russians (in Russia) freely offer unsolicited advice, the authors' study concluded as follows:

> [Russians in Russia] gave more frequent advice than [European Americans] in the context of all relationships except friendships, where the two groups did not differ. Consistent with their bicultural orientation, [Russian Americans] tended to report frequency of advice giving that fell between the other two groups ... A higher percentage of [recent] advice episodes was dedicated to health and practical problems for [Russians in Russia] than for [European Americans].

Trying to explain these differences, the authors speculated that "it is possible that cultures and subcultures that have historically faced chronic failures of formal service structures have fostered similar models of practical interdependence. If so, one would expect to see a similar pattern of results for other post-totalitarian or totalitarian societies, such [as] China, and for subcultures that have historically endured lack of access to formal service structures, such as African Americans." Russians give advice freely, perhaps due to historical shortcomings of government or other formal organizations. Of course, none of this directly impacts cultural differences in advice seeking—our main concern—as opposed to advice giving. Professor Chentsova pointed out to me in email exchanges that it's possible that Russians don't proactively seek high-quality advice, precisely because unsolicited advice is so abundant.

Next let's review research findings about another cultural group: East Asians.

In their 2004 article in the *Journal of Personality and Social Psychology* ("Culture and Social Support: Who Seeks It and Why?"), S. E. Taylor, D. K. Sherman, H. S. Kim, J. Jarcho, K. Takagi, and M. Dunagan reported the results of questionnaires of college students in Seoul, Korea, and in California. Among the students were East Asian students from various countries. The article analyzes support-seeking in response to stress, which is a bit different from advice seeking in response to any issue or problem—our focus—which need not be stressful. The authors wrote:

> Characterizations of Asian cultures as interdependent and Western cultures as independent might seem to suggest that Asians and Asian Americans would be more likely to enlist the help of their social support network in coping with stress, because the self is viewed as fundamentally connected to others ... Similarly, there are compelling reasons to believe that European Americans would be less likely to call on their support networks in times of stress, because in independent cultures, the self is seen as fundamentally separate from others ... hence, those from independent cultures might perceive that they have a personal responsibility to solve problems individually and not through the assistance of others. In contrast to these seemingly self-evident predictions, *the present research revealed exactly the opposite pattern* [my italics].
>
> In three studies, we found that Asians in their home countries and Asians and Asian Americans in the United States reported making less use of social support for coping with stress than European Americans ... cultural norms regarding relationships accounted for the cultural differences

154

in use of social support. East Asian cultural norms appear to discourage the active engagement of one's social support network for help in solving problems or for coping with stress.

This counterintuitive cultural pattern may be explained in terms of how individuals from different cultures value the goals of the self in relation to the goals of relationships. In individual cultural contexts (*e.g., the U.S.*), relationships may be seen as means for promoting individual goals, and as such, one may recruit explicit help or aid from those in one's social networks in order to achieve one's personal goals. In collectivist cultural contexts (*e.g., East Asia*), individual goals may be seen as a means for promoting relationships. Pursuing the goals of the self may risk straining relationships if one calls on his or her social support network for aid ... Thus, a person from an interdependent country may feel that he or she has less to gain personally than he or she can lose socially by calling on others for help. That is, if pursuing the goals of relationships is primary, then a person may prefer not to burden the social network and to solve problems individually instead.

The authors also give examples of how seeking social support can damage an East Asian's social network by "disturbing the harmony of the group, losing face, receiving criticism, and making the situation worse"—the latter because others might become overly worried.

Finally, the authors state, "Latin and Mediterranean interdependent cultural norms may not act to discourage social support use for coping in the same ways that are true of Asian cultural norms."

Chapter 3, "28 Reasons for Not Seeking Advice," mostly drew on examples from a U.S. or Western perspective. There are culture-specific reasons for not seeking advice, such as an East Asian aversion to disrupting the harmony of social networks, or an over-abundance of advice in a Russian culture that freely offers unsolicited advice.

Genetics may even subtly interact with cultural norms. For example, in a 2010 article in the *Proceedings of the (USA) National Academy of Sciences* ("Culture, Distress, and Oxytocin Receptor Polymorphism (OXTR) Interact to Influence Emotional Support Seeking"), the authors H. S. Kim et al. report that Koreans who have a certain gene that is associated with social and emotional connectedness tend to seek social support for managing distress *less than* (repeat: *less than*) Koreans without that gene, whereas European Americans who have the gene seek support *more than* European Americans who lack the gene. Their explanation is that a genetics-based social sensitivity leads interdependent Koreans to go it alone and individualistic Americans to seek help!

Surely more reasons for cross-cultural variation in advice seeking could be uncovered by studying other cultures. It's interesting that these reasons make sense within their context even though they may baffle the outsider. One implication is that informal (unpaid) advisory relations across cultures may operate under wildly different assumptions of what is appropriate.

These cultural variations don't shake my conviction that advice seeking is not practiced often enough nor well enough, but is a universal human good, even if a Russian, Latin, Mediterranean, or Korean guide to advice seeking might be written differently.

This chapter has looked at the fourth landmark of boulders and watering holes present within the advice-seeking terrain that earlier chapters have mapped. Cultural variations in advice seeking can be both boulder and watering hole, since they involve unique obstacles and opportunities. Before arriving at our final destination, the next chapters will mention three well-traveled paths along the terrain that merit some focused commentary.

Chapter 16: What Major Should I Study?

While listening to my goals for this book, two people made valuable suggestions that led to this chapter. My sister pointed out that if I was going to dedicate one chapter to specific problems like recruiting and hiring (see Chapter 18, "Should I Hire This Person?," then I should include a chapter on an even more common problem: deciding what major to study. Separately, a dear friend "Leila" responded to my explanation of the main reasons why people often don't seek advice by telling me the poignant story of how she abandoned her dentistry studies after three years without seeking counsel from anyone, a familiar tale for us by now. I'll quote at length from Leila's self-written history.

> I was 16 when I graduated from high school and it was time to choose my college major. I did not know what to do; I was disoriented, very immature, without plans for the future. I was the type of daughter who didn't give her parents trouble. It has always amazed me that we have to make one of the most important decisions in life when we are still children.
>
> In the country where I grew up, students had to pick their major upon starting college. From the beginning to the end it's the same major. In contrast, the United States has two years of general studies during which the student is deciding his major course of study.

Since I wasn't a good student at that time, I didn't have many career options and colleges to which I could apply. And even if I could choose, I would not have known where to go and what to do. The only career that had crossed my mind, Hospitality and Tourism, had its drawbacks. First, no study center in my city offered it, and second, for my family, that was not a real college major. They didn't consider it a profession and so it was not an option when we discussed my future studies.

Not being a stellar student was not a problem in the small city where I lived, where everyone knew each other and with the right social influence many things could be obtained. My father had a friend who offered to get me admitted to a dentistry school. I was not doing badly in biology, so I just started studying to be a dentist, something I had never thought of. I was happy and grateful to my father because I now had something to study, a dental degree sounded very interesting, and I was making many friends. I was doing well.

My first semester was called Pre-Dentistry. During this semester, the university would weed out some of the students. To keep going, you needed a minimum grade average, which I reached and so continued after my first semester of study to become a dentist.

At that time, my Dentistry school's program of study was largely theoretical during the first two years. Practice on patients began in the fifth semester. While studying theory in the early years, I never thought that dental practice would be a problem.

In my fourth semester, I took a class that began to give me second thoughts: Anatomy Practice. I had no problems with the theoretical part, but the final exam was in the city hospital which had a vat measuring 1 1/2 meters by 3 meters, filled with formaldehyde, which contained many small body parts, such as fragments of a brain or of a lung or liver, all dissected for better study. The exam consisted of the student putting his hand into the vat and pulling out pieces at random, which the student then had to describe to the teacher in detail.

I made a big effort to attend that Anatomy class. I did not like having to dig into a cadaver to find veins, having to take the aorta and carotid and lift them up to show the teacher. Many students enjoyed the exercises; I not so much. During this time I stopped eating meat and my mother was very concerned because I started to lose weight and was losing my appetite.

In my fifth semester we started practicing with patients. The university had a very large dentistry office where students practiced together, with many dentist chairs and a huge list of patients who were generally rural people or indigents who had never been to a dentist. Since the dental services were free, there were many patients. Their mouths were generally in poor condition, with a foul odor which I found disgusting. The first thing we did was the prophylaxis or cleaning, which was much needed. I think that I was not able to do it a second time.

I decided to abandon my studies after my three-year investment. I did not seek any form of advice, did not talk to anybody, I just decided to finish the current semester because I wanted to finish well and show my family that I had a good GPA and was not withdrawing due to bad grades.

I never gave it another try, nor gave anyone a chance to convince me to try again. I did not seek anyone's advice because:

- It just didn't occur to me.
- I did not want to reveal my problems to my classmates.
- I did not know whom to ask.
- I thought they were going to question me so much that maybe I'd change my mind.
- I thought that my family was from another era and would not give me good advice.

Leila's story involved two failures to seek advice: choosing a major in the first place and then abandoning a three-year investment in the major. Many years later, Leila described her situation to dentists and asked what they would have advised her, had she sought them out. She was told that a natural path, if she was set on leaving dentistry, was to parlay her completed years into becoming a dental lab technician, which Leila did not at all consider at the time. Lab technicians provide back-office support to dentists and don't typically see patients.

I repeated this story to my own dentist, who told me a similar story of a dentistry classmate who had been a very smart student but showed little skill working with her hands, even though she was an accomplished pianist. Having always done well at everything else, this classmate dropped out of dentistry school because she couldn't deal with her so-so dexterity compared to her peers.

How common a problem is picking a major? The U.S. Bureau of Labor Statistics keeps data on the educational level of various professions. Citing these statistics, the online *Chronicle of Higher Education* reported that 24.5% of retail salespeople have a college degree, 17.4% of baggage porters and bellhops, 29.8% of flight attendants, and 16.1% of hotel, motel, and resort desk clerks. It's probable that many of them regret their choice of college major, or even regret getting a bachelor's degree, and did not seek out or get much advice during the process.

This book's constant theme is that the best advice takes account of people's circumstances and goals. To say something specific about the problem of "What Major Should I Study?" that goes beyond this book's general recommendations, we can assume this profile of the advice seeker:

- The *circumstances* are those of a young adult who has parents, is literate and Web savvy, and who faces a looming investment of considerable money and time—at least four years of his or her life—in a college major.

- The *goal* is to graduate, although the underlying motives can vary: get started in a well-paying career, become or feel educated, postpone the responsibilities of full adulthood, do what everybody else does, fulfill parental expectations, and so on.

160

Chapter 8, "Who is a Good Advisor?" pointed out a number of qualities that are generally desirable. Advisors should be experienced, discreet, good listeners, serene or unburdened, able to convey reasons and principles, humble, caring (about you), and social. Given our assumed profile of a college-major advice seeker, let's review those qualities.

Good advisors will be experienced, either professionally in general or specifically in the majors you're considering. Experience in a major can include current students, but more valuable is to talk with alumni who studied that major, both those "loyalists" who used that major as a career platform, as well as "defectors" who followed a career path unrelated to the major. Most valuable of all would be to talk with *fellow alumni* who studied the same major in the same college, including both loyalists and defectors.

How to find fellow alumni with a same major? You can search for names of graduates on your college department's Web pages. Alternatively, you can search LinkedIn.com. Go to its Advanced search, type a college name in the School search box, and type the name of a major in the Keywords box, e.g., "criminal justice." Unfortunately, that will match the phrase "criminal justice" appearing anywhere in the LinkedIn bio, not just in the majors studied, but that could lead to interesting matches as well. Then you can contact them. The chances of their responding goes up if you have something in common, such as attendance at the same college. If you are not in college yet nor have other characteristics that you share with them, then you're less likely to get a helpful reply.

You can also try to identify graduates of a major through your parents and their acquaintances, neighbors, teachers, your older siblings and their peers, or the older siblings of your own friends. In the story that starts off this book, Conrad should have asked his scholarship-awarding foundation or his parents to find him an engineer to talk to, even though Conrad's problem was picking a college, not picking a major. In general, older adults are happy to speak about career experiences with young people, but they are rarely asked!

Of the other advisor qualities, being discreet is less important here, unless you're employed and thinking of quitting your job to attend college. Other qualities keep their general importance, but with a few extra remarks. Getting advice from someone who is a recent graduate and unemployed, but not by choice, violates the proverb from an Aesop's fable: "Never trust the advice of a man in difficulties." Their unemployment may be noteworthy for your evaluation, but their analysis of whether their major was a good idea may be clouded by their situation. It's better to enlist the assistance of an unburdened advisor.

Also, since it's better to have humble advisors, in the sense of their not taking offense if you don't follow the advice they give, you should be careful in approaching parents and older relatives for advice if you feel they won't be humble. Don't ask them for solutions but for other types of advice. For example, ask for pointers: "Who do you know that works in criminal justice, or is a lawyer, or studied nursing, etc., that I could speak with?" Or ask about dimensions that you're not seeing, like this: "I'm considering a range of majors; what questions should I consider in trying to come up with a major?" Or even this: "What do you think I'm good at that I should try to leverage in picking a major?"

Friends and relatives of your parents should be good sources of advice, since they are likely to care about you. Also, they can be sources of validation (confidence) and legitimation (support) in case your parents are skeptical about your choice.

Are the faculty *within* a college's departmental major likely to give good advice about whether to study that major? That is, can a political science, computer science, or marketing professor help you to pick political science, computer science, or marketing, apart from inspiring you with their subject-matter teaching and research? In my opinion, not really. College faculty have a tremendous emotional, career, and *life* investment in their field. They even have a self-interest in attracting students to major in it, since their department's funding may depend on the number of students. All this can cloud their objective judgment, no matter how smart they are in their field. As with parents, it's better to ask them other questions than whether you should major in their subject. For example, you could more fruitfully ask, "What are the important emerging areas in your field? What's booming, or going to be booming? What does it take to be successful?"

Let's recall that Chapter 9, "How to Get an Advisor," points out that there is a needs-driven path as well as an advisor-driven path for getting advice. In this case, the needs-driven approach may lead you to seek advisors who can discuss a specific major. On the other hand, the advisor-driven path leads you to approach people who have many of the desirable qualities in Chapter 8, "Who Is a Good Advisor?"—experienced, well-connected, cares about you, and so on—but may lack experience in your specific major.

In all these cases, keep in mind that the advice should pertain to you and to your circumstances and goals. Otherwise it's just canned advice that can be valuable but that needs to be considered in the light of your situation in order to make a good decision. As always, the best advisors should listen and understand you, not just speak about their experience.

As with the problem of whether to change jobs (see Chapter 17, "Should I Change Jobs?"), don't be surprised if you hear contradictory advice. Advisors will diverge due to their distinct experiences within their various professions. They will have different values: Some will think a philosophy major, say, is worthless for business and others will think solid reasoning skills are good training for business careers. Advisors will also differ in the accuracy of their judgments about you in relation to the major. For example, do you need to be good with details in order to succeed in law? Are you good enough in math to study engineering? Will your lack of empathy toward others make you a bad doctor?

Of course, there is much written in books and available over the Web about choosing a major and a career. This fact needs no emphasis here. Don't neglect these sources as background reading.

As Leila's story illustrated, people waste years of their lives studying majors that they end up not liking or not being suitable for. The small experiment of searching the Web for the quoted phrase "didn't like being a lawyer" turned up 165,000 matches on Google. Unfortunately, young people are the *least* likely persons to seek advice proactively, and it is young people who are *most* likely to be in the process of picking a major course of study.

The problem of what major to study is the first of our three well-traveled paths through the advice-seeking terrain that deserve some special commentary. The next chapter will look at the problem of changing jobs.

Chapter 17: Should I Change Jobs?

At one point when I was a college undergraduate, I held two part-time jobs: washing glassware in a biomedical research laboratory, and teaching ESL (English as a second language) to immigrants in Chicago's inner city. The ESL teaching position was with Chicago's City Colleges system and paid $16 per teaching hour, a princely amount in those days. The glassware-washing position paid much less. I decided to quit the teaching position and only wash glassware, without consulting anyone.

At the time, I was teaching ESL at an elementary school in the morning several days per week. Immigrant mothers would drop off their children at school and, instead of returning home, would stay for classes to learn English. My problem was that since the class was open to all comers, I had some students who were barely literate in their native language and others who had university degrees from their home country. Since I generally had high standards for whatever I undertook, I wasn't able to deal with the worry of boring or losing half the class, no matter how I taught.

Was that classroom situation unique? Of course not. However, my own goals and circumstances were special to me. I didn't consult anyone because it didn't really occur to me, as I had not yet formed the habit of actively seeking out knowledge and counsel.

Recalling my circumstances and goals, today I would give the young version of myself advice like this:

- If you quit, the mothers won't be learning English unless/until they hire somebody else. Maybe you're not the best ESL teacher, but you're better than nothing. "The best is the enemy of the good," said the 18th century French philosopher Voltaire, so lower your standards for yourself.

- If the students don't like your class, they'll vote with their feet and not show up, since the class is free to them. If the students keep coming, they must be getting value from the class. So don't worry.

- I know a teacher in an elementary school that doesn't segregate students by ability. I'm sure they have similar challenges. Would you like me to make an introduction for a telephone conversation?

- Have you tried calling your supervisor to explain that the class is going well enough but that you would like to get better, and can you have a talk with the best ESL teacher they have to pick their brain? I know that hardly anyone does this kind of thing and you may find it weird, but since (1) your supervisor should be impressed, (2) the ESL teacher should be flattered, and (3) you'll probably learn something, what's the harm?

- If after trying some of the above, you feel you still can't deal with the stress, then quit at the appropriate time, without regrets. Your main goals right now are to make progress in your studies and earn a little money to help support yourself. If you'll earn less, then spend less or take out a loan.

Taken together, this advice offers solutions, pointers, framing, validation, legitimation, and engagement, the entire package of six benefits described in Chapter 2, "What Advice Does for You." Maybe I would have continued my ESL teaching if someone had advised me like that. Whatever the outcome, I would have made a well-informed choice with no regrets.

Pondering whether to change jobs is a very common problem. For example, a Web search on "should I get another job" got 360,000 matching results, and "should I change jobs" got me 155,000 matches, whereas for comparison, "should I get a flu shot" got only 84,000. In my experience, even mature people quit or switch jobs for emotional reasons, or let frustrations fester until one day they impetuously quit.

This book's general recommendations apply to changing jobs, but one can add several observations that are specific to that issue.

Changing jobs depends on highly individualized factors. Besides your goals and circumstances, which also depend on your education, experience, financial needs, family constraints, commuting distance, opportunities elsewhere, and so on, there are also your co-workers, boss, and employer's circumstances, not only right now but a year or two into the future. Also, many potential advisors have some experience at changing jobs, though not necessarily at their own initiative, but the number of situations they've personally been through are few compared to the many possibilities. All of this, in addition to the high stakes that are involved, begs for high-quality advice from multiple advisors!

Few problems have the potential for as much contradictory advice as changing jobs. Recall the six main sources of contradiction from Chapter 11 "Dealing with Contradictory Advice." They are different experiences, different values, self-interest, perception of your circumstances and goals, misjudgment of the chances of success, and different predictions of the future. All of these come into play along with the limited experience that everyone has in relation to the many possible circumstances. Let's consider the following examples of the six sources of contradiction when giving advice on changing jobs:

- Advisors have different first-hand *experience* with small organizations versus large ones, or nonprofits versus for-profits. Those who are only familiar with one type usually recommend that type. If their idealism has been disappointed, however, they may believe that the grass is greener on the other side of the fence, so they recommend its opposite.

- Some advisors believe in traditional *values* of loyalty to your employer, or to individuals who took a chance in hiring you or are relying on you to complete a project. Others believe that workplace loyalty is obsolete.

- An advisor may have a financial or emotional *interest* in your current employer that biases his judgment. Or an advisor/friend, not wanting to lose your companionship, might not wholly endorse your move to a new city for a great career opportunity.

- Advisors don't always *perceive*, and you haven't told them, that your medium-term *goal* is to follow opportunities and take risks. Or the opposite may occur: Your goal is stable employment that lets you save money to go back to school, buy a house, or start a family. Lacking knowledge of your goals and circumstances, advisors may recommend paths that are unsuited to your true needs and wants.

- An advisor may have thrived in the spontaneous, get-it-done world of small businesses and start-ups and *misjudges* that you will have success there too. Or an advisor misjudges that you will adapt to the more bureaucratic culture of larger organizations, whereas you won't.

- An advisor may *believe*, accurately or not, that one job is with an employer or market segment that will decline—or rise—in the *future*.

Be prepared to hear advice that is all over the map, but don't let that mislead you into getting counsel from only one person.

Younger people will probably have only relatives and same-age peers as readily available advisors, but relatives may not have the right ensemble of qualities, and peers likely will lack the experience. Recall the special cases from Chapter 8, "Who is a Good Advisor?"

- If someone is inexperienced, indiscreet, doesn't listen well, or is burdened, then seek pointers.

- If someone isn't humble, then seek pointers or framing help, but not solutions, unless you know you'll follow their advice, or unless you're not troubled if you don't and they resent it.

Relatives and peers are best asked for pointers and framing help, not recommended courses of action. A referral from them to a solid friend or acquaintance can be valuable.

Chapter 13, "Advice as a Rule, not an Exception," urges closing the loop with advisors to let them know the outcome of your course of action. This is both courteous and builds social capital through engagement. Ideally, you have closed the loop with any previous advisors on career issues; these could be good potential advisors on whether to change jobs. Ideally, they could become career mentors who you can turn to for support and advice over time.

Finally, people often let dissatisfaction mount until they make a largely emotional decision to change jobs. Seeking advice at this late stage is like seeking advice on courses of action when you've already chosen your course. At this point, you're only looking for validation—someone who will confirm for you that you're doing the right thing, giving you the confidence to proceed with no regrets—and life goes on. However, best is to seek advice earlier, when you begin thinking about changing jobs.

In summary, some aspects of advice seeking for the problem of changing jobs deserve special emphasis:

- Getting multiple opinions is *especially* worthwhile because of the limited experience that any single advisor has in relation to the great variety of different circumstances and goals.

- The issue is especially prone to contradictory advice.

- Younger people might not have ready access to good advisors. With mediocre advisors, emphasize pointers (Who can I talk with?) and framing (What am I not seeing? What criteria should I use? What can go wrong?), not recommended solutions.

- Since advisors should know you (and care!), you may have sought advice on previous career issues and closed the loop with them, so you could newly consult them about changing jobs.

- Reach out *early* before you've made up your mind.

Whether to change jobs is a question that arises even more often than the thorny problem of what major to study, so this chapter has dealt with this second of our well-traveled paths along the terrain of advice seeking. In the next chapter, our final such path is a bit different: recruiting and hiring others.

Chapter 18: Should I Hire This Person?

In my nine years as CEO of Vivisimo and in all my years as company Chairman, only once did I get a call inquiring what kind of a job a former employee had done for us (that former employee had done a very good job). Even though Vivisimo had never been a large company during those nine years, and even though its hometown of Pittsburgh has a close-knit technology community, I got only one inquiry. As a small-company CEO and founder, I could be considered an expert on the performance and attitudes of many former employees. If I had no personal knowledge, however, I had ready access to experts, that is, to the former employees' direct supervisors. Why didn't prospective employers inquire?

Many people don't consult past employers because they don't know how to go about it or they think it's a waste of time. A typical sentiment that I found on the Web:

> I work for a small, family-owned retail store. When people apply to work there, the job application form asks for three work references. My boss (the owner) insists that she can't call the references because they are forbidden by law from telling her anything useful, and therefore it's a waste of time.

At the back of his *The 7 Habits of Highly Effective People*, author Stephen Covey was asked the following: "If you had to do it over again, what is the one thing you would do differently as a businessperson?" His answer:

I would do more strategic, proactive recruiting and selecting. When you are buried by the urgent and have a thousand balls in the air, it is so easy to put people that appear to have solutions into key positions. The tendency is to not look deeply into their backgrounds and patterns, to do "due diligence," nor is it to carefully develop the criteria that needs to be met in the particular roles or assignments. I am convinced that when recruiting and selecting is done strategically, that is, thinking long-term and proactively, not based upon the pressures of the moment, it pays enormous long-term dividends. Someone once said, "That which we desire most earnestly we believe most easily." You really have to look deeply into both character and competence because eventually, downstream, flaws in either area will manifest themselves in both areas. I am convinced that although training and development is important, recruiting and selection are much more important.

Inquiring about prospective employees or business partners is a special case of seeking advice, with its standard expectations, cultural practices, and even legal obstacles, so it deserves this small chapter of its own. Few advice-seeking professional situations are as widespread or even as important as adding another employee to a small company or to a small group within a larger company, or adding a high-level employee to a company of any size.

Let's examine the constraints that the advice seeker operates under. They include the following:

- Common business ethics dictates that one does not contact anybody at the candidate's current employer (if there is one) unless the candidate gives explicit authorization to do so. If contacting the current employer is authorized—which is the less usual case—it's often because the employer is downsizing or because the candidate has informed the employer that he or she will be moving on.

- Laws that govern references vary by state in the United States. Generally, you are not allowed to ask questions of a reference that you would not be able to ask of the candidate, such as questions relating to race, religion, expectations of pregnancy, and so on. I am not a lawyer, so I'll leave it at that.

There are other legal or liability constraints on what the reference or advice giver is allowed to say. However, our focus here is on the *advice seeker*.

The ultimate goal is figuring out whether to recruit or hire a candidate, but the criteria vary greatly depending on what you're looking for, and the appeal of what it is you have to offer. The common thread, as with most of this book, is that advice seeking for hiring, better known as background or reference checks, is not done well or not done at all. But it's important, and it's possible to teach how to do it better in a book.

I have always been an enthusiastic background checker, because I realize its tremendous importance for the well-being of a small company, and because I relish the entrepreneurial challenge: Starting from scratch, figure out with some confidence and in a short time, with the entire outside world as one's potential resource, whether a candidate is right for a job. I'll discuss a few of the techniques I've used, largely learned from others.

The first target of the background check is of course the candidate himself or herself! We need advice from the candidate on his suitability, not so much by asking the trite "Why are you right for this job?" but by hearing stories about similar situations the candidate has been in. What are those similar situations? Not those that are narrowly just like what your organization does, but rather aspects that are common to all careers: transitions, goals, and accomplishments. Jack Welch, the former longtime CEO of General Electric, wrote in his book *Winning* that the single most informative question to ask is this, in my adapted and expanded version: "For every place you've been (starting with college, say), why did you go there, what was your mission, who was your supervisor, what did you accomplish, and why did you leave?"

Hearing the candidate's career story can take a long time, but it's crucial "advice" for you, since it reveals the candidate's personal goals, how the candidate acts on those goals, if the career transitions made sense or were due to other reasons that might recur in your own company, if the candidate's accomplishments aligned with the mission, and so on. Be sure to state that you're in no hurry. And bring glasses of water for the two of you to sip, since you'll be sitting and listening to the candidate for a while!

Another valuable question is: "What's the biggest mistake you ever made?" Everyone makes mistakes, so one is looking for whether they identify a mistake that they themselves were responsible for. Some candidates state instead that their biggest mistake was not realizing that their co-workers or teammates were not up to the job, or failing to convince their supervisors about a right course of action. In both cases, other people are wrong, and one's biggest mistake is not being able to cope effectively with a co-worker's incapacity. These are not great answers and are suggestive of an overgrown sense of entitlement. It is better to honestly identify a mistake that oneself caused.

The follow-on question is: "What did you learn from this mistake?" Jointly, these questions probe whether they are capable of admitting mistakes to themselves and others, of diagnosing the reasons for the mistake, and of adjusting their future behavior appropriately. These are excellent character habits, but not all people have been taught them.

The other source of "advice" is people who have worked with the candidate before. As already mentioned, if the candidate is currently employed, ethics prohibits calling on references that aren't explicitly provided by the candidate. But often the candidate is not currently employed, is known to be on his way out, or is forthcoming with references anyway. I've found the following technique to be very useful.

First, explain that you are an open book, and that the candidate should feel free to inquire about your history with anyone you've been associated with, even if not everything they hear will be positive. (Of course, if you have many skeletons in your own closet, then this method isn't for you!) They are generally surprised and pleased to hear this, and frequently say so. Then you ask: "Do you mind if I do the same in your case?" If they are not employed, they can then hardly say no if you have already given them the same privilege. If they are employed, then they will explain their circumstances and the constraints they are under, which you must respect. The goal is to not be limited to contacting the references that they supply, which will usually be positive or perfunctory. If you had the candidate walk you through his career as recommended above—Who did you report to in each position?—then you have a ready-made list of people to contact if you have permission. Finding people is easy via Web search engines, national electronic phone directories, LinkedIn, etc.

If the position being recruited for is important, it's valuable to talk with co-workers: peers, supervisors, or subordinates who weren't designated by the candidate. Here's an easy method: While finishing a reference call, ask who else knows the candidate well, then give them a call. Also, if the candidate has worked at a small company or small department within a larger company, then LinkedIn can reveal co-workers who overlapped with the candidate during their mutual employment. In these cases of approaching people without an introduction, it's best to state up front, during a message or on a live call, who you are and why it's very important for you and for the success of your project to conduct this background check, which may be seen as extraordinary since most people don't do this. More than once I've left messages at homes after looking up names in the public phone directory, figuring that it's a free country and the worst that can happen is that I'm simply ignored. You can't rely on outside recruiters to be this zealous, since the stakes aren't as high for them. Using these techniques of *guerrilla reference checking*, I've personally dodged more than one bullet, dropping candidates who presented an appealing façade that disguised a shaky foundation that could have toppled our efforts.

Despite your best efforts and techniques, some former associates or supervisors don't give much useful information, even when you've succeeded in reaching them. To deal with this problem, I often employed a method that I read somewhere: Call a reference when they are unlikely to answer the phone, for example, at 6 p.m., preferably using your company's phone so they can verify who is calling them. Leave a message explaining why you are calling and say, "If you think so-and-so did a good (or great) job for you, I would very much appreciate a call back at [give your mobile phone number] at your convenience, day, night, or weekend." The reference then has no excuse for not calling you, since you've signaled the importance of the matter by supplying your personal mobile number and asking to be called back at any time. Importantly, you have given the reference an option not to call back at all if the candidate didn't do a good or great job. If you leave one message and don't get a call back, there remains the doubt of whether the reference is on vacation, sick, didn't get the message, or whatever. But if you do the same with five people, then no or few calls back will tell you something.

As with any advice, it is both courteous and excellent practice to "close the loop" with the advice givers, also known as background references, especially in the case of candidates who went on to join your organization. A brief email or voicemail that says you're closing the loop, you are grateful for the help, and that you are reporting the outcome to them—a successful hire—will always be appreciated and will help build the relationship for any future needs.

Finally, I wish to describe a piece of hiring advice that I gave and of which I am especially proud, although it concerns interviewing, not hiring. After remaining at Carnegie Mellon as a research faculty member, I learned from the inside how time-consuming the faculty recruitment process is. College departments recruit assistant professors from a fresh batch of Ph.D.s or of recent Ph.D.s who did a stint at a temporary position of one, two, or even three-years. The top-tier departments, armed with their prestige and resources, often have success at hiring top talent. However, second- and third-tier departments have challenges: They would like to hire very good talent, but they can't tell if the talent will be scooped up by a higher-ranked department with which they can't compete on prestige and resources. A nightmare scenario is that a lower-tier department gears up for hiring after having been authorized to do so by university administrators, forms a recruiting committee, schedules candidate visits, interviews candidates, deliberates on the available options, makes one or more offers, and then is rejected by the candidates, leaving nothing to show for six months of work along with a budget slot that could be yanked if not filled. The horror! Given this inside picture of how things might work, how should candidates adjust their approach, putting themselves in others' shoes? Let's next consider an example from my personal experience.

I had lunch with a friend who was just finishing his doctorate and was interviewing locally for a position as assistant professor. I asked him if he wanted to stay in our local area, and he confirmed that he did. I then recommended that at an appropriate time, when speaking with the head of the recruiting committee, he should tell them this: "I would like to stay in this area, so if you offer me a position, I will accept it." My friend was surprised, since his inclination was to play hard-to-get, behavior that would imply that he was in demand and so would be a good catch. I asked him to look at it from the recruiter's viewpoint, and in particular to consider the nightmare scenario of doing lots of administrative recruiting work, which is a distraction from the productive work that all faculty prefer to do, and being left with no hire at the end of the process. He could remove all of that uncertainty with a single forthright sentence. As it turns out, my friend did as I advised and was offered the position, which he accepted. Of course, because he was an outstanding candidate, the result likely would have been the same whether he'd made the statement or not, but it was a good move nonetheless. Knowing the circumstances and goals of the advice seeker—the recruiter in this case—you can provide a key piece of advice: Offer me the position and I'll accept it.

Finding the right people to hire involves proactive advice seeking, as illustrated by the story of recruiting a VP of engineering in Chapter 10, "How to Set Up an Advice Process." Once good prospects are identified, advice is needed from the prospects themselves as well as from people who relied on them professionally in the past. Some techniques are specific to this task, but otherwise deciding whom to hire is just another example of leveraging the expertise of others.

This chapter has looked at the third of our well-traveled paths through the terrain, viewing the problem of whether to hire a job candidate using the lens of advice seeking. At this point, we have accomplished many tasks: surveyed the landscape, read the scouting reports, built our own map, heeded interesting landmarks, and chronicled some noteworthy paths that many people traverse. The next and final chapter will accompany us to the destination.

Chapter 19: Get Advice and Prosper

Having arrived at our destination, and assuming this book has fulfilled its promise, you should now be able to notice new productive and fulfilling paths to follow, paths that would have stayed unseen if we had jetted to the destination, unaware of the rich terrain below, instead of hiking and taking it all in.

Let's summarize what we've learned:

1. Most people are not proactive about seeking advice, or are not very skilled at it, so they *go it alone* and needlessly make inferior decisions.
2. No matter how smart you are about an issue, somebody else out there is smarter, with few exceptions. Find them.
3. Advice consists of much more than just solutions to your problem. It contributes pointers, dimensions, validation, legitimation, and social engagement.
4. Knowing that advice is more than just recommended solutions, and that authority figures sometimes take offense if you don't follow their solution, you can better leverage their knowledge by asking for pointers, dimensions, and validation, staying away from discussing solutions.
5. There are many reasons for avoiding advice, from lack of imagination, to the emotional, cultural, and even biological factors that come into play. Usually these reasons aren't good enough. They should be overcome.
6. There is a cultural undercurrent of extreme self-reliance, as reflected in the U.S. by Emerson's and Thoreau's writings. It's not effective and it's pointlessly heroic. Better to emphasize effectiveness and to

succeed—achieve one's goals—through collaborative self-improvement.

7. People often heed or disregard advice for non-rational reasons: allure, status, or reputation of the advisor, the advisor's success in areas that are totally irrelevant to your issue, and so on. It's helpful to be aware of these in order to avoid them.

8. Try to avoid preferring a course of action before you've gotten advice, because having a favorite will cloud your judgment.

9. A consensus profile of the best advisors is that they are experienced, untroubled, humble, caring, able to convey principles and not just specifics, and advise only when called upon.

10. Good advisors will want to listen to you in order to understand your goals and circumstances before they offer advice.

11. Good advisors are precious. Show courteous deference, meet with them at their convenience, and close the loop with them by letting them know the outcome of your process.

12. Contradictory advice is a fact of life, but it's not the only place where contradiction exists, since everything from folk wisdom to leading-edge scientific knowledge is filled with principled disagreement that is totally without malice.

13. Try to understand the sources of contradiction: differing experience and values, misunderstanding of your circumstances and goals, self-interest, misjudgment of whether an advisor's experiences transfer well to your situation, and different views of what the future holds.

14. Use the Web and social media for background reading, for finding potential advisors, and to prepare for meetings. Don't rely on the Web and social media exclusively for advice if your problem involves unique individual circumstances and goals.

15. Make advice seeking a habit. Never let "I didn't think of it" be a reason for not seeking advice.

16. Elite schools of scientific research are culturally very advice-intensive, which accounts for much of their success in breeding new, productive scientists. It's worth understanding how they operate.

17. Habits of advice seeking and advice taking vary across national cultures. In some cultures, people might avoid seeking advice not because they are socially inept but because they are socially attuned and want to avoid disrupting their harmonious relationships by involving others.

18. It helps to view recruitment and hiring of new employees and business associates as a special case of advice seeking. The task is to creatively get knowledge about whether candidates are a match, including from the candidates themselves.

19. Tremendous time and money are wasted in studying majors that are ill-suited to an individual. Much of the waste could be avoided by getting advice beforehand.
20. Advice seeking is a form of social engagement that provides benefits that go way beyond the immediate problems to be solved.

As promised in Chapter 1, on problems that can benefit from careful thought, the principles and methods set forth in this book will help you do the following:

- *Think of* getting advice.

- Decide if seeking it is worthwhile in this case.

- Figure out who are good advisors.

- Do background research.

- Approach advisors productively.

- Engage with them in human terms.

- Evaluate their counsel.

- Choose the best courses of action with more confidence.

- *Not* agonize every step of the way.

Advice is not for pipsqueaks and losers. Advice is for winners. Everyone can learn to do it more often and better, and thereby make better decisions at work and in life. May you get good advice and prosper!

20443159R00105

Made in the USA
Lexington, KY
10 February 2013